ECOLOGY A TO Z

BY PAUL FLEISHER

 **DILLON PRESS**
New York

Maxwell Macmillan Canada
Toronto
Maxwell Macmillan International
New York   Oxford   Singapore   Sydney

For my nieces and nephews:
Chris, Keyontae, Retea, Valmiki, Jessica,
Nandi Devan, and Michael

Acknowledgments

The author would like to thank Tresa Fleisher, Toni Manning, Frederic March, and Joyce Stanton, as well as Kelly Kyle, Anne Repp, and Lisa Hill of Richmond's Narnia Bookstore, for their assistance in the completion of this work.

Photo Credits

Cover courtesy of Priscilla Connell-Photo/Nats

S. C. Delaney/U.S. EPA: 13, 70; C. Michael Lewis: 22; David M. Stone-Photo/Nats: 25; Don Johnston-Photo/Nats: 46; Tim McCabe/U.S. Department of Agriculture: 53; Chesapeake Bay Foundation: 78; Jo-Ann Ordano-Photo/Nats: 103, 179; U.S. Department of Agriculture: 110; Debbie Needleman: 120; U.S. Windpower, Inc.: 214.

Book design by Carol Matsuyama
Illustrations by Patricia Keeler
Photo research by Debbie Needleman

Library of Congress Cataloging-in-Publication Data

Fleisher, Paul
    Ecology A to Z / by Paul Fleisher. -- 1st ed.
      p. cm.
    Includes index.
    Summary: Provides information about terms, from "abiotic" and "floodplain" to "oil spill" and "zooplankton," related to a wide range of environmental concerns.
    ISBN 0-87518-561-4
    1. Environmental sciences--Encyclopedias. Juvenile. [1. Environmental sciences--Encyclopedias.] I. Title.
GE10.F57 1994
363.7'003--dc20   93-13623

Dillon Press   Maxwell Macmillan Canada, Inc.
Macmillan Publishing Company   1200 Eglinton Avenue East
866 Third Avenue   Suite 200
New York, NY 10022   Don Mills, Ontario M3C 3N1

Macmillan Publishing Company is part of the Maxwell Communication Group of Companies.

First edition

Printed in the United States of America

10 9 8 7 6 5 4 3 2 1

CONTENTS

INTRODUCTION

The earth is covered with an amazing layer of living creatures. There are millions of different kinds of plants, animals, fungi, and microbes living on our stony planet. Life has adapted to survive in every imaginable spot on earth's surface, from the ice of Antarctica to the driest desert to the volcanic vents at the bottom of the ocean.

But no creature can survive on its own. Every living thing depends on a complex web of other creatures for food, oxygen, and even shelter. Each living thing also needs the non-living parts of its environment to survive—things like water, sunlight, and mineral nutrients. The study of these complicated connections between each creature and its surroundings is called ecology.

Ecology is a fascinating branch of the life sciences. It lets us take a peek into how life on earth works. It shows us how living systems maintain their balance and how individual species adapt to their surroundings. It lets us glimpse the endless connections between one creature and all the others living around it.

Ecology is important for another reason: The human race is facing a grave environmental crisis. People are rapidly changing the ecological balance of our planet. We have been more successful than any other species in using the earth's natural wealth. Our population is still expanding and we are using more and more of those resources. We're so successful that many other species are being crowded out and forced toward extinction.

As we've used the planet's resources, we've been careless about the waste we've produced. Some of that waste is deadly to other creatures and to ourselves. We've abused, poisoned, and polluted the very environment that we depend on for our lives.

The world's human population is still growing, but the world's resources are limited. The earth's minerals and farmland, the fish and forests, the coal and fresh water are all there

4

is. We can't make or borrow more when they run out. Sooner or later, our planet won't be able to support all the people living on it. Then we'll be faced with unimaginable hardship and disaster.

The earth's temperatures are rising—a result, scientists believe, of too much carbon dioxide produced by burning fossil fuels. In many places, the air and water are badly polluted. Waste gases are damaging the ozone layer. In some parts of the world, fertile land is turning to desert. The world's forests are being cut down at a rapid rate. In many parts of the world, food, fuel, and water supplies are already desperately scarce. At the same time, others of us use much more than we really need.

Fortunately, our species has a powerful weapon on our side—our intelligence. Our intelligence has helped us spread across the planet. It has let us learn to use its resources. Now our intelligence can help us learn to use those resources wisely.

Perhaps we still have time to show that we understand that our lives depend on a healthy, balanced environment. We can learn that when we damage the environment, we damage our own life-support system. We can protect our planet's limited resources and remember not to waste them. We can remember that our well-being depends on the well-being of all the other species in the complex web of life. And we can remember that each individual action we take has an effect on the world around us.

In some small way, I hope this book will help with that process of learning, so that we humans can continue to survive and prosper on this beautiful planet.

A

Abiotic

Abiotic means nonliving. Many important parts of the environment are abiotic. For example, air, water, minerals, heat, and sunlight are all abiotic factors in an ecosystem.

Abyssal Zone

The abyssal zone is the region of the ocean's deepest trenches. In some places the ocean is more than five miles deep. No light from the sun reaches this zone. The water temperature is just a few degrees above freezing, and the pressure is more than a thousand times greater than at the ocean's surface.

Because there is no light, plants can't survive at these depths. Animals that live in the abyss have evolved unusual methods of coping with the harsh environment. For example, many are bioluminescent—they produce light with their own body chemistry. This light is useful in attracting prey or attracting a mate.

Abyssal creatures can't survive the lower pressures at the surface, so they are difficult to study. Scientists are just beginning to discover the wonders of this unusual environment.

Acid Mine Drainage (see MINING)

Acid Rain/Acid Precipitation

Normal rain or snow is slightly acidic. It has a pH (the measure of acidity) of about 5.6. Precipitation with a pH less than 5.6 is considered acid rain. Acid rain can have a pH as low as 4.0 or even lower. That's more than 15 times the acidity of normal rain.

Air pollution includes the chemicals sulfur dioxide and nitrogen oxides. These gases are produced when fuel is burned in cars, power plants, furnaces, and factories. The gases become strong acids when combined with moisture in the air. When the moisture condenses to form rain, the rain is acidic, too.

Acid rain is especially bad in certain regions, such as the northeastern United States and Canada, and northeastern Europe. That's because the winds that cross these areas have picked up pollution from industrialized and heavily populated regions nearby.

Acid rain harms animal and plant life. Some lakes in New England and eastern Canada are now so acidic that fish can't live in them. Acid rain also kills or slows the growth of trees and other plants. Some plants can't get the nutrients they need from acid soil. Plants weakened by acid rain are more likely to be killed by insects or disease. Acid rain even damages buildings and statues made of metal or stone.

Acid rain can be controlled in several ways. Adding lime to streams and lakes temporarily lowers the acidity of the water. Cleaner burning fuels produce less acid-causing air pollution. Burning less fuel and using fuels more efficiently also helps. Putting emission-control devices on smokestacks, chimneys, and car exhausts also lowers the amount of acid-causing pollution that gets into the air.

Adaptation

An adaptation is a change in a genetic, or inherited, trait of a species of plant or animal. This change makes the creature more successful in its environment. Adaptation is the way a species adjusts to changing environmental conditions.

For example, over many centuries the birds that originally settled in Hawaii have adapted to take advantage of the different foods there. Some species developed long, probing beaks to drink nectar from flowers. Other developed beaks of different shapes to catch insects or to crack seeds.

Adaptations take place over many generations. Organisms with short life spans can adapt more quickly than those with longer ones. Many insect pests have been able to adapt to new insecticides in just a few years. That's because insects go through several generations in a single season.

Creatures can't adapt to sudden, massive changes in their environment. There's not enough time. That's one reason why the huge ecological changes that humans create have caused other species to become endangered or extinct (*see* EVOLUTION).

Aeration

Aeration means adding air to soil or water. Aeration of the soil causes plants to grow better because the roots can get more oxygen and nitrogen compounds. Earthworms aerate the soil with their digging, as do some insects and mammals, such as prairie dogs and field mice. Farmers aerate the soil by plowing and tilling.

Aeration is also important for water environments. It provides oxygen for the organisms living in the water. Streams are aerated as water tumbles over rocks and waterfalls. The action of waves helps aerate large bodies of water, such as lakes and oceans.

Aeration is also one of the methods used to purify drinking water and to treat sewage. Aerating drinking water adds oxygen and removes other dissolved gases that spoil the water's taste. Aeration gives sewage-digesting bacteria the oxygen they

9

need to break down wastes in wastewater treatment plants.

Aerobic

Aerobic means using oxygen. Most organisms have aerobic metabolism, or body chemistry. They take in oxygen and use it to change food into energy. The main waste products of these chemical reactions are carbon dioxide and water.

There are a small number of organisms that generate energy with different chemical reactions and without oxygen (*see* ANAEROBIC).

Aerosol

An aerosol is a fine spray of tiny droplets or particles. Smoke and fog are examples of aerosols.

Hair spray, deodorants, foods, paint, insecticides, and many other products are sold in spray cans that dispense their contents as aerosols. These aerosol sprays are forced out of their cans with pressurized gas, called the propellant.

Aerosol spray cans were invented in 1941. By themselves, they are not necessarily harmful. But some propellants harm the earth's environment. In the past, aerosol cans used Freon as a propellant. We now know that Freon damages the earth's ozone layer. Freon is now banned as a propellant in many countries (*see* CFCS).

Some modern spray cans use butane gas as a propellant. Butane doesn't destroy ozone, but it does add to the greenhouse effect (*see* GREENHOUSE EFFECT). Butane also burns. Other spray cans use harmless nitrogen gas as a propellant.

Aerosol cans also create a lot of solid waste. Once they're empty, they can't be reused. To solve these problems, some companies sell hand-pumped aerosol spray bottles. These products need no propellant, and they can be refilled and reused.

Agent Orange

Agent Orange was the name of a chemical herbicide widely used in the 1960s and early 1970s by U.S. forces in the Vietnam War. Agent Orange was sprayed from planes. It was used to kill jungle vegetation, so that North Vietnamese and Viet Cong soldiers would have fewer places to hide. It was also used to kill crops.

Agent Orange contained chemicals, including dioxins, that were toxic to people as well as plants. The U.S. destroyed its remaining supplies of this chemical warfare agent in 1977. Veterans exposed to the spray claim to have developed skin rashes, nerve disorders, cancer, and other long-term health problems. Little information is available on the effects of Agent Orange on the people and wildlife living in the sprayed areas.

Agriculture

Agriculture is farming—growing crops and raising livestock. Agriculture feeds and clothes most of the earth's human population. Farming is one of the most dangerous occupations. Farmers work with heavy machinery and many hazardous chemicals. Agriculture also has a great effect on the earth's environment.

Even the best farming methods force people to compromise between human needs and the need to protect the environment. A plot of land is completely changed by farming. It must be cleared of trees, shrubs, and grasses. Wild animals living there are displaced or killed. The land is plowed, and a single crop replaces the hundreds of different plants that lived there before. Modern farmers often use chemical fertilizers and pesticides.

The environmental effects of farming reach far beyond the farmland. Rain washes topsoil from the plowed land into rivers and streams. No longer held in place by the roots of trees and plants, topsoil is also carried away by the wind. Farm chemicals can pollute the environment. Farm machines burn large amounts of fossil fuels.

Farmland is a limited resource. Only about 11 percent of the world's land is suitable for agriculture. The rest is too cold, dry, or mountainous. Much of this same land is also attractive for other uses, such as housing or industry. Some of the best farmland in the United States has been lost to urban development.

Air Pollution

Air pollution is the smoke, dust, fumes, and other contaminants that dirty the air and are harmful to life.

The main sources of air pollution are automobile exhaust, furnaces, fumes from industry, fires, and agricultural spraying. Major air pollutants include carbon monoxide, fine particles, oxides of sulfur and nitrogen, ozone, and certain organic compounds such as unburned fuels that remain in automobile engines.

Air pollution harms the lungs and eyes of animals and people. Air pollution also damages plants, including farm crops. Plants along highways are often stunted because of exhaust fumes. Air pollution causes acid rain and even damages buildings made of stone and steel.

The simplest and most common method of handling air pollution is dilution. That means mixing the pollutants with large amounts of fresh air. But dilution doesn't really solve the problem. It just spreads it out.

There are other ways that air pollution can be controlled. These include putting emission-control devices on chimneys, smokestacks, and auto exhausts; building more efficient engines and furnaces; using nonpolluting solar and hydroelectric power; and passing laws that set high standards for emissions and automobile efficiency.

Industrial fumes are a major source of air pollution. Using emission-control devices on smokestacks helps reduce the amount of pollutants released into the atmosphere.

Alaska Pipeline

The Alaska pipeline is an 800-mile pipe that carries petroleum from the oil fields in northern Alaska to the port of Valdez on the state's southern coast. The pipeline is four feet in diameter and can carry over 80 million gallons of petroleum each day. For about

13

half its length, the pipeline is built above the frozen ground. The Alaska pipeline is just one of many thousands of pipelines that carry petroleum and other products around the world.

Workers began building the pipeline in 1974. It was completed in 1977. It was one of the biggest jobs ever undertaken. People were worried that it would harm the Alaskan environment. Would it leak oil and pollute the tundra? Would the warmth of the flowing oil disturb the life cycles of local wildlife? Could the pipeline withstand earthquakes? What effects would all the extra workers have on the Alaskan wilderness? Engineers tried to design the pipeline to limit harm to the environment.

Although the pipeline itself has had no major failures as of 1993, there was a major environmental disaster connected with the Alaska oil industry in 1989. That year the tanker *Exxon Valdez* struck a rock in Prince William Sound and spilled 11 million gallons of crude oil into Alaskan waters.

Alga; Algae (plural)

Algae are the simplest green plants. Algae grow in fresh and salt water and in damp soil. Some species of algae are single-celled and microscopic. Others, such as kelp and other seaweeds, grow very large and are made of many cells. Algae reproduce by cell division or by producing spores. They do not produce seeds.

Algae produce much of the earth's food and oxygen. The world's oceans are full of algae—not just seaweeds but also huge numbers of microscopic floating algae called phytoplankton. Like other plants, algae use sunlight to produce oxygen, sugars, and starches. Because they need light, algae can only live near the surface of the water.

Algae provide food for the many tiny animals at the base of the food chain. Some seaweeds are also harvested for human food or are processed into thickeners for foods, paints, cosmetics, and many other products.

Algal Bloom

An algal bloom is a rapid growth of algae in a pond, lake, or ocean. It occurs when conditions become ideal for algae growth. When temperatures are right and there are lots of nutrients in the water, microscopic algae grow and divide very quickly. Algal blooms often happen when fertilizer or detergents wash into ponds or streams. These pollutants provide extra nutrients that help the algae grow rapidly.

An algal bloom provides lots of food for animals that feed on the tiny plants. But it can quickly become an environmental problem, too. Algae grow until they use up the nutrients. Then they start to die. The tiny animals feeding on the algae die also. As the dead organisms decompose, they use up the oxygen in the water. This kills off many animals living in the water.

Some saltwater algae also produce poisons as they grow. When these species bloom—an event known as red tide—the poisons become concentrated enough to kill fish and shellfish. People who eat seafood gathered during a red tide can become ill.

Anaerobic

Anaerobic means without air or oxygen. Most living things use oxygen to turn food into energy. But a few organisms have different metabolisms (body chemistries). These creatures have adapted to live in environments where little oxygen is available. They generate energy with other chemicals—usually sulfur compounds.

For example, anaerobic bacteria live in the mud of marshes and swamps. Almost no air gets into the dense, wet mud. The bacteria there must live without oxygen. When the mud is turned over, there's a strong sulfurous smell and a black color characteristic of anaerobic microbes. Another anaerobic bacterium, *Clostridium botulinum*, can grow in improperly canned food, producing a deadly toxin.

Recently anaerobic organisms have also been found living near volcanic vents at the bottom of the ocean. These strange clams, worms, and other creatures use the sulfurous chemicals from the underwater volcano as their source of energy.

Appropriate Technology

Appropriate means suitable. Appropriate technology is any method suited to the resources, climate, and culture of a particular region of the world. This term can be used to describe farming techniques, energy generation, or methods of transportation, and construction.

What's appropriate in one part of the world may not be suitable somewhere else. For example, large tractors are fine for the huge farms in Illinois or Kansas. But they aren't appropriate for small family plots in India or Southeast Asia. It wouldn't make sense to help farmers in those regions by giving them tractors. A Rototiller or draft animals to pull a plow would be much more useful and appropriate.

In the past, the United States and other Western countries tried to help the people of developing nations with complex, high-tech projects. These projects often failed. Now aid agencies try to give assistance that is less complicated and better suited for the people who will use it and the places where it will be used.

Aquaculture

Aquaculture is farming of fish, shellfish, and water plants. Aquaculture provides more than 10 percent of the world's seafood.

Aquaculture is often done in saltwater or freshwater ponds. Depending on what species is being grown, aquaculture can also take place in tanks, marshes, areas of water surrounded by nets, or even in the open ocean. Species grown with aquaculture include shrimp, clams, oysters, catfish, trout, carp, and even edible seaweeds.

People have used simple forms of aquaculture for thousands of years. But many aquaculture methods are still quite new or even experimental. Since over 70 percent of our planet is covered with water, aquaculture could become an even more important source of food in the future.

Aquifer

An aquifer is a natural underground layer of sand, gravel, or porous rock that holds groundwater. Rainwater feeds an aquifer. The rains trickles down through the soil and slowly makes its way into the slow-moving underground river or lake.

The place where an aquifer comes to the earth's surface is called a spring. Wells tap into aquifers for drinking water and for irrigation.

Aquifers can become polluted just as surface streams can. When landfills, underground tanks, or toxic dumps leak, their poisons can leach into the groundwater. Because the water in an aquifer moves very slowly, the pollution also spreads slowly. Once an aquifer becomes polluted, it is very difficult to clean up, because the water is deep underground.

Aquifers can also be overused. For example, much of the drinking and irrigation water in the southwestern United States comes from aquifers. As more people have come to live in this region, they've used more and more water. The water table (the level of the water in an aquifer) has dropped. Wells have to be drilled deeper, and water use has to be limited. Unless they conserve water, people in this region face serious water shortages.

Aral Sea (*see* IRRIGATION)

Asbestos

Asbestos is a soft, fibrous mineral. It has been widely used for insulating and fireproofing. It was used for many years in ships, public buildings, and homes. Many schools were built with asbestos insulation in walls, ceilings, and around pipes. It is still used in brake linings, cements, fire-resistant fabrics, and caulking.

Unfortunately, asbestos fibers in the air can cause asbestosis and lung cancer when inhaled. It takes many years before symptoms appear in people who have been exposed to asbestos. The asbestos that once provided safety is now known to be a serious pollutant. In 1973, the U.S. Environmental Protection Agency banned it in schools. Two years later it was banned in all public buildings.

Since then, billions of dollars have been spent to remove or safely cover up the asbestos in public buildings. And more has been spent to care for

18

workers who became sick from breathing the fibers in the air where they worked.

Asexual Reproduction

Asexual reproduction is the production of new individuals without the combining of male and female cells (sperm and egg). Single organisms of many different species can reproduce themselves this way.

Organisms reproduce asexually in various ways: In cell division, a single-celled creature like an amoeba divides itself into two smaller but complete creatures. In budding, a small "daughter" organism grows on the side of the parent organism. When it is completely formed, it drops off and begins an independent life. Many plants reproduce asexually by sending out shoots, runners, or underground stems that grow into new plants.

Many organisms reproduce both sexually and asexually at different stages in their life cycles.

Atmosphere

The atmosphere is the layer of gas surrounding a planet. Earth's atmosphere is the mixture of gases we call air. Air is about 78 percent nitrogen and 21 percent oxygen. The other 1 percent includes argon, carbon dioxide, water vapor, helium, hydrogen, and tiny amounts of other gases. The atmospheres of other planets are very different.

The atmosphere is held in place by gravity. The larger the planet, the thicker and denser its atmosphere. Because of gravity, the atmosphere is densest near the surface of a planet. The farther you get from the center of the planet, the thinner the atmosphere becomes. Three to four miles above the earth, the air is too thin for people to breathe and

19

survive for extended periods.

Scientists divide earth's atmosphere into layers: The troposphere is the layer closest to the earth's surface. It extends about 10 miles. Almost all the earth's weather occurs in the troposphere. The stratosphere lies 10 to 30 miles above the earth. The ozone layer is located in the stratosphere. Above the stratosphere are other layers where the air is extremely thin.

Life on earth depends on the atmosphere, of course. Plants and animals need oxygen from the air for respiration (breathing). Plants need carbon dioxide for photosynthesis, the chemical process that produces starches and sugars. Damage to the atmosphere—air pollution—causes serious problems for earth's living things.

Atoll

An atoll is a ring-shaped island made of coral. Atolls develop where an undersea volcanic mountain is just below the ocean surface. Coral, a type of sea animal, grows on the underwater peak. When each coral dies, it leaves its hard limestone shell behind for other corals to grow on. Gradually the coral builds a low, ring-shaped island around the mountaintop. As the mountaintop wears away, all that remains at the ocean's surface is the ring of growing coral.

Automobile

The first gasoline-powered automobiles were invented in the late 1800s. Since then, the automobile has changed the way people live. There are now about 350 million cars on earth. Most are in North America, Europe, and Japan.

Automobiles are wonderfully convenient. But they are also our worst source of pollution. They burn billions of gallons of gasoline each year and belch out huge amounts of polluting exhaust. They use nonrenewable energy resources, and compared to other forms of transportation, they don't use fuel efficiently.

Cars allow people to live far from where they work and shop. As a result, cities have spread farther and farther into the surrounding countryside.

Cars are also responsible for many deaths and injuries. Thousands of people are killed and millions are injured in auto accidents each year. Many animals are killed as well.

The problem of automobile pollution has no easy solutions. But here are some changes that could help:

- Safer, more efficient cars that use less energy and burn fuels more cleanly

- Cars that run on other energy sources, such as electricity, natural gas, or hydrogen

- More laws to limit the amount of pollution that cars produce

- More recycling of old automobile parts into new products

- City planning that limits the need for people to drive long distances to work, play, or shop

- Car pooling, so each auto carries more people, and planning automobile trips to avoid unnecessary driving

• Better mass transit systems, such as buses, trolleys, subways, and trains

This solar racing car was built by high school students in Peterborough, New Hampshire. In a competition the car won awards for speed and energy efficiency. The electrical energy it uses is equivalent to 500 miles per gallon of gasoline.

"Away"

When we are finished with something, when it becomes trash or garbage, we "throw it away." But in a broader view, there *is* no "away." The earth is a closed system. Except for a few space probes, nothing really goes away.

Humans produce large amounts of toxic wastes. Even when that waste is buried deep in landfills or dumped in the deepest ocean trenches, we haven't really thrown it "away." It's still somewhere in our planet's ecosystem. Many of the recent environmental disasters our world has experienced are the result of poisons that were thrown "away" coming back to affect us (*see* KEPONE, LOVE CANAL, TIMES BEACH).

Bacteria

Bacteria are microscopic, single-celled organisms. They are neither plants nor animals. They are considered part of the kingdom Monera—simple one-celled creatures that lack a distinct nucleus. Instead, their genetic material is found throughout the cell.

Bacteria reproduce rapidly by dividing. A single cupful of soil or pond water can contain millions of bacteria. Bacteria are a necessary part of any ecosystem. They are decomposers. Bacteria break down dead plant and animal matter and release nutrients. They are also food for many other small organisms.

Different kinds of bacteria have different functions. Bacteria living on the roots of some plants, like beans and peas, change nitrogen from the air into the nitrates that the plants need to grow. Others break down decaying material. Bacteria in the guts of animals aid in the process of digestion. Some bacteria cause diseases in plants and animals.

Bangladesh

Bangladesh is a small Asian nation located just east of India, where the Ganges River enters the Indian Ocean. It became an independent country in 1971. Much of Bangladesh is at or just above sea level and is subject to flooding. Bangladesh is also one of the world's poorest countries. Most of its overcrowded population survives by farming small plots of land.

Because of Bangladesh's poverty and its geography, it has had several huge environmental disasters. In 1970, a hurricanelike storm called a cyclone killed about 250,000 people. Since then, other storms and flooding have killed many thousands more and left millions homeless. In 1991, another cyclone flooded 300 miles of Bangladesh's lowlands and killed more than 100,000 people. Other disasters are almost certain to happen in Bangladesh in years to come.

Barrier Island

Barrier islands are long, low islands that form along sandy ocean coastlines. Barrier islands start as sand-bars built up by ocean waves. After a while, the sand forms a low island. Wind piles the sand into dunes. Plants take root on the island, making it more stable. Barrier islands protect the land and waterways behind them from ocean waves. Salt marshes often form in these protected areas.

People often live on barrier islands or use them for recreation. Coney Island in New York City; Atlantic City, New Jersey; and Nags Head, North Carolina, are all built on barrier islands.

Because they're made of sand, barrier islands are always changing shape. Wind and waves carry sand away from one part of the island and deposit it somewhere else. This constant change causes problems for people who build homes and roads on them. Seawalls and jetties help keep ocean waves from washing buildings and beaches away. But storms still cause property damage on barrier islands every year. A large storm can even wash away an entire island or destroy everything that has been built on it.

Beach Erosion

Beach erosion is the washing away of beach sand by the action of wind and waves. Beaches are always eroding in some places and being built up in others. It is a normal, natural process. Beach erosion is most severe during heavy storms.

Beach erosion becomes a human problem when people build homes and businesses on waterfront property (*see* BARRIER ISLAND).

A beach in Cape Cod, Massachusetts, badly eroded by a blizzard. A portion of a parking lot was also washed away.

Benthic Zone/Benthos

The benthic zone, or benthos, is the habitat at the bottom of a lake, bay, or ocean. This is the home of animals such as clams, oysters, burrowing worms, and many other bottom dwellers, including fish such as flounder.

Some benthic creatures are scavengers, eating the dead plants and animals that sink to the bottom. Others are filter feeders, gathering tiny particles of food as they strain the water with their mouths or gills. Still others are predators, hunting the other creatures that live on the bottom.

Bhopal, India

Bhopal, a city in central India, was the site of one of the world's worst environmental disasters. In 1984 there was an explosion in a pesticide factory owned by the Union Carbide Company. A huge cloud of methyl isocyanate, a deadly gas, was released. No one is certain what caused the explosion.

The gas killed about 2,500 people and injured another 200,000. Many of the injured were burned or blinded by the gas. The Indian Supreme Court ordered Union Carbide to pay $470 million to the victims. That money, however, couldn't begin to repair the human damage the disaster caused.

Bioaccumulation

As nutrients are passed up the food chain, so are poisons. Some chemicals stay in an animal's body long after they are taken in with food, air, or water. This process is known as bioaccumulation. Poisons like DDT, PCBs, lead, and mercury are just a few of the many substances that bioaccumulate.

As an animal eats, drinks, or breathes more of such chemicals, their concentration builds up in its body. When a predator eats the animal, the poisons then enter the predator's body. A bioaccumulating poison may be found only in tiny amounts in the water or soil of an environment. But it becomes thousands of times more concentrated in predators at the top of the food chain. That's why even low levels of pollution in the environment can have disastrous effects on birds of prey or other large predators.

For example, suppose that insects have been sprayed with a pesticide. A frog eats many insects, so the pesticide becomes more concentrated in its body. A bass eats many frogs, concentrating the poison even further. When an eagle catches and eats the bass, it is concentrated yet again.

Biodegradable

Anything that is biodegradable can be broken down by bacteria, fungi, and other decomposers. Dead plants and animals, food wastes, leaves and grass clippings, and paper and cardboard are all biodegradable. Biodegradable wastes can decompose in landfills or compost heaps, or if they're just left to rot on the ground.

Much of the solid waste that people produce is not biodegradable. Metal, glass, and most plastics don't decompose. They remain intact for hundreds or thousands of years. Recycling trash that isn't biodegradable helps reduce the problem of overflowing landfills. Some companies have also begun producing plastics that are biodegradable to help with this problem.

Biodiversity (*see* DIVERSITY, BIOLOGICAL)

Biological Clock/Biorhythm

Seeds germinate in the spring. Trees drop their leaves every fall and birds "know" when to migrate. Animals mate and reproduce only at certain times of the year. A biological clock, or biorhythm, is any of these daily, monthly, or yearly patterns in the natural world. Daily biorhythms are known as circadian rhythms.

Biological clocks are regulated by sunlight, temperature, moisture, and other factors in an organism's environment. For example, gardeners know that spinach and radishes are spring crops. The plants go to seed as summer approaches and the days get longer. Tomato plants won't produce fruit until the nighttime temperatures are above 65°F. The exact workings of many biological clocks are still a scientific mystery.

Biological Pest Control

Biological pest controls are methods that repel or

27

kill insects or other pests by using diseases, predators, or natural repellents.

For example, gardeners can use ladybugs to control aphids. Ladybug larvae eat many of the destructive sucking insects. Gardeners also use *Bacillus thuringensis,* a germ that kills many crop-destroying caterpillars, such as cabbage worms. Ranchers use dogs to guard livestock from predators.

Releasing large numbers of sterile male insects is another form of biological pest control. Farmers may release thousands of male fruit flies, sterilized with radiation, near their crops. These males mate with females. The females then lay unfertilized eggs that cannot develop into a new generation of flies.

Some gardeners even grind hot peppers into a liquid and spray it on their plants to repel damaging insects.

Most biological controls don't destroy pests as completely as insecticides do. They have the advantage, however, of controlling pests without the use of poisons.

Biological Warfare

Biological warfare is the use of disease-causing microorganisms such as bacteria, viruses, or fungi as weapons of war. Biological warfare was outlawed by a United Nations treaty in 1972. Nevertheless, many nations including the United States have experimented with these deadly microorganisms and with methods of spreading disease to enemy territory. This kind of research is usually done in secret; it is likely that a few nations are still conducting research into the use of biological weapons (*see* WAR).

Biology

Biology is the branch of science that studies life in all its many forms.

Biomass

Biomass is any organic material—wood, leaves, sawdust, grain, or even garbage—that can be changed into energy. The big advantage of biomass energy is that it is renewable: More can be grown to replace what is used. Biomass is essentially solar energy stored in biological materials.

Biomass can be turned into energy simply by burning it. It can also be changed into fuels like alcohol, methane, or synthetic oil. For example, grains or wood pulp are fermented and then distilled into alcohol.

Biome

A biome is an ecosystem that covers a wide geographic area. Climate is the most important factor that defines a biome. Each biome has characteristic plant and animal species adapted to it.

The earth's major terrestrial (land) biomes include tundra, desert, tropical rain forest, grassland, temperate deciduous forest, temperate coniferous forest, northern coniferous or boreal forest (also known as taiga), chaparral, and savanna. The ocean environment also contains several different biomes.

Bion

A bion is any living organism.

Bioremediation

Bioremediation is the use of microbes to break down and clean up wastes in the environment. Bioremediation is widely used as a part of wastewater (sewage) treatment. In large aerated tanks, bacteria digest much of the solid waste in sewage before the treated wastewater is returned to the environment (*see* WASTEWATER TREATMENT).

Bioremediation is also used to clean up oil spills and some toxic wastes. For example, scientists have found bacteria that feed on petroleum products, PCBs, and toxic herbicides such as 2,4-D. Researchers are looking for bacteria that can break down other poisons, and are trying to create new, useful varieties of bacteria through genetic engineering.

Toxic spills cannot be cleaned up simply by spreading bacteria on them. Ordinarily, bioremediation must be done in tanks or containers supplied with extra air to help the bacteria grow.

Biosphere

The biosphere is the thin zone of the earth's surface where life exists. The biosphere includes the top layer of the earth's rock and soil; the oceans, streams, rivers, and lakes; and the lower layer of the atmosphere.

Biota

Biota are the living organisms found in a particular environment.

Biotic

Biotic is an adjective describing living organisms. Plants, animals, fungi, and bacteria are all biotic elements of an environment.

Birth Control

Preventing pregnancy, or limiting the number of offspring that people or animals have, is known as birth control.

There are many different methods of human birth control. These include abstaining from sex, sterilization, birth control pills, and various birth control devices, such as condoms and intrauterine devices (IUDs).

The world's human population is growing faster than our planet's ability to support us. This is a grave problem: We can't improve the lives of earth's people or preserve its resources unless our human population stabilizes. That's why birth control is such an important ecological issue.

Birthrate

The birthrate is the number of births in a given year for every 1,000 people. The current birthrate in the United States is about 16 births per 1,000 people each year. In some countries, it is much lower; in others, it is almost twice as high.

When the birthrate of a population is higher than its death rate, the population increases. Almost everywhere in the world, the birthrate is higher than the death rate. The earth's human population is growing by about 1.6 percent each year. At this rate, the population is growing by about 90 million people each year. In 1993 the world's population was about 5.5 billion. Scientists predict that if current trends continue, it will reach 10 billion by the year 2050.

Bog

A bog is a kind of wetland. Bogs have wet, spongy soil with poor drainage and few nutrients. The soil and water in a bog are naturally acidic. A bog may have deep layers of decomposing plant material—called peat—below its surface. Peat is sometimes dried and used for fuel.

Bogs don't have a wide variety of plants living in them. Mosses and grasses are the most common. Some bog plants, like sundews and pitcher plants, capture insects. There are so few nutrients in the soil and water that these plants survive by trapping and digesting insects.

Boreal Forest (*see* TAIGA)

Broad-Spectrum Pesticide

A broad-spectrum pesticide is one that kills a wide range of different organisms rather than targeting a specific pest. The danger of broad-spectrum pesticides is that they also kill harmless and beneficial species along with the pests.

Sevin is an example of a well-known broad-spectrum insecticide used in home gardens. It kills a variety of insects that damage garden plants. But Sevin also kills honeybees and earthworms, which are valuable in any garden.

BTU (British Thermal Unit)

The BTU is a measure of energy. It represents the amount of heat needed to raise the temperature of one pound of water by 1°F. One BTU is equal to 252 calories. BTUs are most often used to measure the energy value of fuels.

Calorie

A calorie is a measure of heat energy in the metric system. A calorie is the amount of heat needed to raise the temperature of 1 gram of water exactly 1°C. Calories are used to measure the energy value of food or fuels.

Camouflage

Camouflage is any adaptation that helps an animal stay hidden in its environment. Camouflage makes an animal less likely to be seen by predators, and so less likely to be eaten. Predators may be camouflaged to keep hidden from their prey.

Some animals camouflage themselves by adopting the colors of their environment. Snowshoe hares, for example, turn white in winter so that they are hard to see in the snow. Fish are countershaded—dark on top and almost white underneath. This makes them less visible to predators from both above and below.

Other animals are camouflaged with markings that help them blend into the environment. The tiger's stripes make it less visible in the dappled shade of the forest. Animals even take the shape of objects in their environment. For example, some insects look like the twigs, leaves, or thorns of the plants they live on.

Cancer

Cancer is the name given to a large group of diseases. In these diseases, some of the body's cells grow out of control, forming a tumor. If discovered

early enough, many cancers can be treated by removing the tumor or by stopping its growth with
powerful drugs or radiation.

Many cancers are caused by substances in the
environment. These cancer-causing pollutants are
called carcinogens. Asbestos, cigarette smoke, radon, plutonium, and ultraviolet radiation are just a
few of the thousands of carcinogens that researchers
have identified.

Once a chemical has been found to cause
cancer, it is usually controlled by government
regulation. Scientists are still studying how and
why cancer cells develop and grow. The causes of
many cancers are still unknown. Since cancers often
take many years to develop, finding the causes can
be very difficult. Cancer-causing chemicals may
not be identified and controlled until after they've
affected many people.

Carbohydrates

Carbohydrates are a group of chemical compounds
that include sugars, starches, and cellulose. They
are the main source of food energy for all plants and
animals. Carbohydrates are made of carbon, hydrogen, and oxygen atoms.

Plants make carbohydrates in the process of
photosynthesis. Plants use the energy in sunlight to
turn water and carbon dioxide into carbohydrates.
Carbohydrates are a plant's way of storing solar
energy for later use. Animals use this energy, too,
when they digest the carbohydrates in the plants
they eat.

Carbon Cycle

The carbon cycle is the process by which carbon and
its chemical compounds move through the living

and nonliving parts of the environment.

Plants take carbon dioxide from the air and turn it into carbohydrates by photosynthesis. Eventually, the plant dies. As it decays, the carbon is released back into the atmosphere as carbon dioxide. If the plant is eaten, the carbon is released as carbon dioxide when the animal exhales or when it dies and decomposes. In either case, the carbon returns to the air to begin the cycle over again.

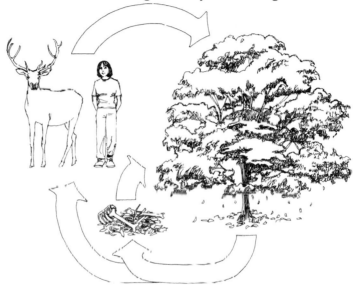

Carbon Dioxide

Carbon dioxide is one of the gases in earth's atmosphere. It is clear, colorless, and odorless. A carbon dioxide molecule is made up of one carbon atom and two oxygen atoms. Its chemical formula is CO_2.

Carbon dioxide is formed when material that contains carbon (such as coal, oil, or wood) is burned completely. CO_2 is also produced when people and animals breathe and when plant and animal matter decays.

Carbon dioxide only makes up about 0.035 percent of earth's atmosphere. However, this small amount is very important because plants use it to make food. Plants take CO_2 from the air during photosynthesis and change it into carbohydrates.

Carbon dioxide is also a greenhouse gas. CO_2 in the air traps some of the sun's heat in the atmosphere instead of allowing it to radiate back into space. This is the main cause of global warming. As people burn more fuel and cut down more forests, the amount of carbon dioxide in the air increases. There is about 25 percent more carbon dioxide in the air now than there was two centuries ago. This increases the greenhouse effect, and may cause the earth's climate to become warmer (*see* GLOBAL WARMING, GREENHOUSE EFFECT).

The United States produces about one quarter of all the world's CO_2 emissions. In the early 1990s, the nations of the world began working on agreements to limit the amount of CO_2 they produce.

Carbon Monoxide

When carbon compounds burn without enough oxygen present, carbon monoxide gas is formed. A carbon monoxide molecule is made up of one carbon atom and one oxygen atom. Its chemical formula is CO.

Carbon monoxide is odorless, colorless, and poisonous to breathe. It prevents blood from carrying oxygen to the cells of the body. Carbon monoxide is a pollutant found in automobile exhaust. It is also in smoke, including cigarette smoke.

Carbon monoxide itself can burn, so it is sometimes used as a fuel for cooking and for heating. Bad-smelling chemicals are added to the carbon monoxide so that people will notice a gas leak immediately.

Carcinogen

A carcinogen is any substance that causes the body to develop cancer. Cigarette smoke, for example, contains carcinogens. Asbestos is another example of a carcinogen (*see* CANCER).

Carnivore

A carnivore is a meat eater—an animal that eats other animals. Cats, dogs, sharks, wolves, and hawks are all carnivores. Carnivores are also known as secondary consumers. Primary consumers eat plants directly. Secondary consumers get their food from plants indirectly, by eating other animals that have gotten their food from plants. Some secondary con sumers, known as omnivores, eat plants as well as other animals (*see* HERBIVORE, OMNIVORE).

Carrying Capacity

An ecosystem can provide food and shelter for only a limited number of creatures. That upper limit is called the carrying capacity of an ecosystem. Carrying capacity depends on how productive the ecosystem is. The more productive it is, the larger its carrying capacity.

Productivity in turn depends on how much energy (such as sunlight) and nutrients are available. An estuary has a very high carrying capacity, for example. Sunlight provides plenty of warmth and energy for growing plants, and the rivers feeding into the estuary provide lots of plant nutrients. Tundra, on the other hand, has a very low carrying capacity. It gets little sunlight for much of the year, and its thin layer of thawed soil has few nutrients to support plant growth.

Carson, Rachel

Rachel Carson (1907–1964) was an American marine biologist and author. In 1962, her book *Silent Spring* made the U.S. public aware of the dangers of pesticides in the environment. It described the damage that pesticides were doing both to wildlife populations and to people. The book had a huge worldwide impact and helped start the modern environmental movement.

Carson is also known for three books on the ocean environment: *Under the Sea Wind* (1941), *The Sea around Us* (1951), and *The Edge of the Sea* (1954).

Catalytic Converter

A catalytic converter is an air pollution control device used in the exhaust systems of cars. The converter helps complete the combustion of any fuel that was not burned in the engine. It changes the unburned hydrocarbons and carbon monoxide in the exhaust into carbon dioxide and water vapor. The converter uses chemical catalysts, usually platinum and palladium, to create this change.

Catalytic converters became standard equipment on U.S. cars by 1975. Modern wood-burning stoves and heaters also use catalytic converters.

Cats

Cats are common household pets in the United States and throughout much of the world. There are about 60 million cats living in the United States. Some of them are abandoned and live as wild animals.

Cats are predators; even if they are well fed, they hunt and kill other animals by instinct. Cats kill hundreds of millions of small animals each year, including birds, small mammals, lizards, and frogs.

When they were introduced to remote islands by human settlers, cats helped kill off a number of native species.

In the United States, naturalists consider cats a threat to some species, especially songbirds. To limit this problem, cat owners can control their pets and make sure they are spayed or neutered to keep cat populations from growing.

Cattle (*see* MEAT)

Census

A census is a population count. A census can be taken of animals or plants, as well as of human populations.

CFCs (Chlorofluorocarbons)

CFCs are a family of chemicals that contain atoms of both chlorine and fluorine. The most commonly used CFC is called Freon. Most CFCs are gases at room temperature. They are odorless, nontoxic, nonflammable, and chemically stable.

CFCs have important uses. Freon is used as a refrigerant in freezers, refrigerators, and air conditioners. CFCs are also used in fire extinguishers because they don't support burning. Until recently, CFCs were also used as propellants in aerosol spray cans.

Unfortunately, CFCs also harm the atmosphere. When refrigerators and air conditioners leak or break, or when someone uses a CFC fire extinguisher or a spray can with a CFC propellant, CFCs get into the air. There they cause damage to the earth's ozone layer.

Ozone in the upper atmosphere protects us from the sun's ultraviolet radiation. But the chlorine and fluorine from a single CFC molecule destroy hundreds of ozone molecules. CFC molecules also trap heat, adding to the greenhouse effect and global warming.

In 1978 the U.S. government banned most uses of CFCs as aerosol propellants. In 1987 a treaty to limit the use of CFCs was signed by 31 nations. The United States is scheduled to stop production of CFCs by 1995. The law now requires refrigeration mechanics to recycle CFCs instead of releasing them into the atmosphere.

Scientists are now looking for other, less damaging refrigerants that work as well as CFCs.

Chaparral

Chaparral is a dry, semidesert region populated with shrubs and small trees. It is one of the earth's major biomes. Chaparral is found in western North America, southern Australia, Chile, and around the Mediterranean Sea. Chaparral has long, hot, dry summers and mild, damp winters.

Fires are common in the chaparral's dry season. Many chaparral plants depend on fire to help their seeds spread and germinate. In North America, animal species of the chaparral include mule deer, bobcats, quail, rabbits, and lizards. Plants include manzanita, scrub oak, California laurel, and sparse grasses.

Chemical Warfare

Chemical warfare is the use of poisons to kill or disable people. Some herbicides, which kill crops or forest land, are also used as chemical weapons (*see* AGENT ORANGE). Chemical weapons may be sprayed from planes or dispersed with bombs or missiles.

During the 20th century many countries developed arsenals of chemical weapons. Poison gases were widely used in World War I. In 1993 a United Nations treaty banned the production, stockpiling, and use of chemical weapons. The treaty also included strict methods to assure that nations which sign the treaty follow its rules. The United States and Russia are still in the process of destroying their stockpiles of chemical weapons. It is likely that some nations still maintain arsenals of chemical weapons despite the treaty (*see* WAR).

Chernobyl

Chernobyl is a town near Kiev in Ukraine, a part of the former Soviet Union. Several nuclear power plants are located near the town. In 1986, one of these reactors exploded and caught fire. The reactor was destroyed and huge amounts of radioactive material were released into the environment. It was the worst nuclear reactor accident in history. It released more radiation than the atomic bombs exploded over Hiroshima and Nagasaki at the end of World War II. Radiation spread through the atmosphere and was detected around the world.

It took weeks for workers to control the leaking radiation, and months before the entire reactor was buried in a concrete tomb. In the meantime, 130,000 people were evacuated from a 300-square-mile area. Dozens of workers who battled the reactor fire later died of radiation poisoning. (No one is sure of the exact numbers.) Hundreds of others became sick. The radiation from the reactor will cause thousands of cancer deaths over the next several decades. For example, childhood thyroid cancers have increased 80 times in neighboring Belarus since the Chernobyl disaster. Some areas around the reactor are still uninhabitable, and a large

41

region around Chernobyl is too contaminated to be used for agriculture.

Chlorinated Hydrocarbons

Chlorinated hydrocarbons are a group of chlorine-containing chemicals, many of which are poisons and carcinogens. A number of them have been used or are used as insecticides. These chemicals include DDT, aldrin, dieldrin, chlordane, and heptachlor.

The Environmental Protection Agency has either banned or strictly limited the use of these pesticides in the United States. Many of them bioaccumulate—they remain in the body of an animal that consumes them, accumulating over years at the top of the food chain in predators like trout, bass, raccoons, eagles, and ospreys. Chlorinated hydrocarbons were a major reason for the decline in the populations of hawks, eagles, and other predatory birds in the United States. Human deaths have also been caused by improper use of these poisons.

PCBs are another group of chlorinated hydrocarbons that have caused serious environmental damage (*see* DDT, PCBS).

Chlorine/Chlorination

Chlorine is a chemical element. It is a yellowish green poisonous gas. Chlorine is chemically very active. It combines rapidly and sometimes violently with many other chemicals. Chlorine compounds have many important industrial uses. They are used in insecticides, bleaches, cleaning fluids, and refrigerants (CFCs). Chlorine is used to kill germs in drinking water and swimming pools, and to treat wastewater. The process is called chlorination.

The use of chlorine is a good example of the

compromises people must make with environmental hazards: Treating drinking water with chlorine saves many thousands of human lives. It's the best way to prevent deadly waterborne diseases like cholera and typhoid fever. But chlorine-treated water itself is slightly hazardous. People who drink chlorinated water have a slightly higher risk of getting bladder or rectal cancer. The danger of getting sick from untreated water is much worse than the cancer risk from treated water. But there is a trade-off. People must accept one kind of environmental threat to remove another.

Chlorofluorocarbons (*see* CFCS)

Chlorophyll

Chlorophyll is the green pigment in plants. It is one of the most important substances on earth. Green plants use chlorophyll to produce food in the process of photosynthesis.

Chlorophyll is a large, complex molecule. When it absorbs the energy of sunlight, a complicated chemical reaction begins to change water and carbon dioxide into carbohydrates (sugars and starches) Oxygen is also given off as a by-product of this reaction.

Cigarette Smoke

Cigarette smoke is a common indoor air pollutant. Tobacco smoke contains poisons, including carbon monoxide and cyanide, that prevent the blood from carrying oxygen to the body's cells. It also contains nicotine, an addictive poison that increases heart rate and blood pressure. Tobacco smoke can cause lung cancer, emphysema, bronchitis, and other lung diseases. Smoking causes 30 percent of all U.S. cancer deaths and 20 percent of all deaths from heart disease.

Tobacco smoke is also harmful to nonsmokers. Nonsmokers who are married to smokers have higher lung cancer rates than spouses of nonsmokers. Babies of mothers who smoke have twice as many lung infections as other babies. Smoking costs many billions of dollars each year in health care costs and lost work time.

In recent years, the government has limited cigarette advertising. Smoking is not allowed in many public places. The number of smokers in the United States is dropping, but the habit is spreading in other parts of the world. Millions of people still pollute their own lungs with this habit.

CITES (Convention on International Trade in Endangered Species)

The Convention on International Trade in Endangered Species is a treaty first signed in 1973. By 1990 more than 100 nations had joined. Signers agreed not to buy or sell endangered species of plants and animals or products made from them, such as furs, hides, and ivory. Despite this treaty, some endangered animals are still killed by poachers and sold to customers willing to pay high prices for them.

Clean Air Act

The Clean Air Act is a law first passed by the U.S. Congress in the 1960s. Since then the law has been expanded and toughened several times. It is intended to reduce or limit air pollution and acid rain.

The Clean Air Act sets air-quality standards for sulfur dioxide, ozone, carbon monoxide, CFCs, and other air pollutants. It requires cities and states to test their air. They must control auto emissions, regulate industries, and even promote car pooling in order to lower pollution.

The most recent Clean Air Act sets deadlines for U.S. cities to meet clean air standards. It sets limits for the amount of pollutants that power plants can produce. It also allows factories that clean up below their allowable level to sell part of their pollution allowance to another factory. That permits the other factory to continue polluting at high levels. Not surprisingly, this part of the law is unpopular with environmentalists.

Clean Water Act (see FEDERAL WATER POLLUTION CONTROL ACT)

Circadian Rhythm (see BIOLOGICAL CLOCK)

Clear-cutting

Clear-cutting is a method of harvesting trees for lumber or wood pulp. In clear-cutting, all trees in a section of forest are cut down and removed. After cutting, the area is replanted with new saplings, or it may be left to regrow naturally.

Clear-cutting can be very destructive to the environment. It removes nutrients that would otherwise be returned to the soil when trees die and decompose. It destroys habitat for wildlife. Clear-cut areas may also erode because there are no trees to soften the force of heavy rains and no tree roots to hold topsoil in place. The soil is then washed into nearby streams, causing pollution.

Supporters of clear-cutting say it is more efficient than selective cutting. Young trees grow much faster than older, mature ones. An acre of fully grown forest produces less wood per year than an acre that has been cleared and replanted with new, young trees. Clear-cutting also requires the use of less energy for machinery and transportation. It disturbs fewer acres of woodland than selective cutting. Brushy young growth makes a better habitat for some animal species, too (*see* FORESTRY, SELECTIVE CUTTING).

Clear-cutting timber can result in the loss of topsoil. The muddy runoff from clear-cut areas also pollutes nearby streams, killing fish and other wildlife.

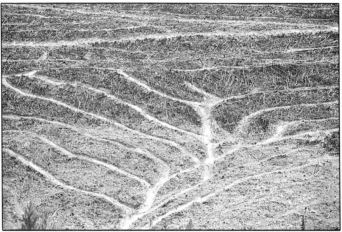

Climate

Climate is the prevailing, or usual, weather conditions of an area. Climate includes such things as temperature, rainfall, winds, humidity, and barometric pressure.

Climate is one of the most important abiotic factors in an environment. The kinds and numbers of creatures that live in any environment depend on its climate. Hot, moist climates, such as that of the tropical rain forests, have many more different species than dry or cold regions, such as desert or tundra.

Climax Ecosystem

An ecosystem is the group of plants and animals living together in an environment, along with the physical factors that support them. A climax ecosystem is one that is in the final stages of an ecological succession. Ecosystems change in a predictable, orderly way. This process is known as succession. Fields become overgrown with weeds, then shrubs, and then young trees. Gradually what once was a field becomes a mature forest. A climax ecosystem is the final step in that succession. Once an ecosystem has reached the climax stage, it is usually stable and changes very little unless it is disturbed.

A mature forest is just one example of a climax ecosystem. The plant and animal growth that develops over several years on a piling in an estuary is another example of a climax ecosystem. Eventually, the entire piling is covered with mature plant and animal life—seaweed, oysters, barnacles, crabs, and many other creatures.

There are also areas of climax growth in the tundra, in the desert, on rocky shorelines, and in all the other biomes of the world.

Coal

Coal is a fossil fuel. It was made over millions of years, as dead plants were pressed beneath layers of sedimentary rock. Coal is mainly carbon, combined with rock and sulfur compounds. When it is burned, the sulfur becomes polluting sulfur dioxide gas, and the rock is left behind as ash.

Coal is a nonrenewable resource. The world's supplies of coal were made many millions of years ago. Once these supplies are used up, they cannot be replaced. At current rates of use, it's estimated that the world has at least 200 years of coal left. China, the United States, Russia, and Eastern Europe all have large coal reserves. Coal mining damages large areas of the earth's environment. It is also one of the most dangerous occupations.

In addition to being used as solid fuel, coal can be changed into liquid or gaseous fuels. It is also used to make dyes, solvents, and medicines.

Cogeneration

Cogeneration is an energy-saving method of producing, or generating, electricity and heat at the same time. In one method of cogeneration, fuel is used to turn water into high-temperature, high-pressure steam. The steam turns generators, creating electrical power. Then the same steam is used to heat nearby buildings. This process gets more energy value from the same amount of fuel.

Other cogeneration plants use the hot exhaust of burning fuel to turn a gas turbine, much like a jet engine. The turbine turns a generator to produce electricity. The hot gases from the turbine are then used to heat buildings.

Cogeneration plants are usually smaller than the centralized plants of the big power companies. This has made it possible for some manufacturing companies to build their own cogeneration plants to provide heat and power to their buildings. Such factories often sell the extra power they generate back to a large power company.

Commensalism

Commensalism is a one-sided relationship between two different species. In commensalism, one species benefits from the association; the other species is neither harmed nor helped.

One example of a commensal relationship is the pea crab and the oyster. The tiny soft-shelled pea crab lives inside an oyster's shell. The shell protects the crab, and the crab gets a steady supply of food from the water that the oyster draws into its shell. The crab does the oyster no harm, but it doesn't help it, either.

Another example is the feathery gray-green Spanish moss that grows on tree branches throughout the southern United States. The tree branches support the moss and allow it to receive more sunlight than it would get if it were on the ground. The trees are neither helped nor harmed by this hitch-hiking plant.

Community

No individual or species can survive by itself. Each species, each individual, depends on its community—a complicated web of other living things. A community is a group of organisms that live together in a habitat.

Organisms in a community rely on one another in many ways: Plants provide food and oxygen for animals in the community. Prey animals provide food for predators. Scavengers and decomposers clean up the community by eating dead animals and plants. Plants provide shelter for many small creatures. One animal may dig a hole or grow a shell that another animal later uses for a home.

Compaction

Compaction is tight packing of soil that happens as farm machinery rolls over fields year after year. A compacted layer of soil called hardpan forms just beneath the top layer of soil that is regularly plowed and tilled.

Hardpan makes it more difficult for plants to grow. Roots don't penetrate the layer easily, so plants get fewer nutrients. And hardpan keeps rainwater from draining through the soil, creating puddles where plant roots can't get enough oxygen.

Soil compaction also can be seen along any trail. Where people or animals have walked, the soil is more tightly packed. Plants grow poorly along compacted trails, even when there is very little traffic.

Compaction can also refer to the crushing of trash so that it takes up less space in a landfill.

Competition

There are only limited supplies of water, nutrients, sunlight, shelter, and other resources in any ecosystem. Living things must compete to get these scarce resources.

Competition takes place between different species and between individual members of a species. Organisms use many different strategies to compete for scarce resources. For example, some plants—trees—grow very tall to gather as much sunlight as possible. Other plants—vines—climb upward to reach sunlight. Some plants, like the creosote bush, even produce chemicals that poison other nearby plants so that they have the sunlight to themselves.

Compost/Composting

Compost is decayed organic wastes—grass clippings, leaves, and kitchen scraps, for example. It is produced by the action of decomposers like bacteria and fungi. Compost is rich in nutrients.

Gardeners often use compost to fertilize their gardens, returning nutrients to the soil. Compost also improves the soil's ability to stay moist. And composting reduces the amount of waste that would otherwise be sent to landfills.

Some municipal waste treatment plants also

compost sewage sludge or yard wastes before returning them to the environment.

Comprehensive Environmental Response, Compensation and Liability Act (CERCLA)
(*see* SUPERFUND)

Conservation

Conservation means protecting and saving natural
resources. Almost no natural resource is unlimited.
Some resources, such as water, trees, or stocks of
seafood, are renewable. But these resources can be
overused or damaged. Conservation of renewable
resources involves using them wisely, so that they
last.

Other resources, such as petroleum, coal, mineral ores, and even wilderness areas, cannot be re-
newed. Once they are used, they're gone forever.
Conservation of these resources means using as little
of them as necessary, and making the most of what
we do use. It also means finding renewable resources
to take their place, if possible.

There are many different ways to conserve resources. Recycling, energy conservation, establish-
ing parklands, wilderness preservation, regulating
hunting and fishing, planting trees, contour plowing to prevent soil erosion, and disposing of dangerous household wastes properly are just a few of the
ways people can practice conservation.

Consumers

Consumers in an ecosystem are animals. They consume, or eat, the food that is produced by plants.

Primary consumers eat plants directly. Deer,
rabbits, beavers, grasshoppers, and carp are all

primary consumers. Secondary consumers are predators. They don't eat plants directly. Instead, they eat animals that depend on the plants for food. Wolves, lions, praying mantises, and trout are examples of secondary consumers.

Directly or indirectly, all consumers depend on the ability of plants to make food by photosynthesis. Without plants, the consumers would have nothing to eat.

The word *consumer* also refers to human beings as they use goods and services (see next entry).

Consumption

Consumption is the use of goods and services, including energy and raw materials. As consumers, we buy and use food, clothing, cars, appliances, homes, electricity, gasoline, medical care, movies, and thousands of other products and services.

U.S. citizens use far more than their share of the world's resources. For example, the United States has only 5 percent of the world's population but consumes about 25 percent of the world's energy. In general, people in industrialized nations consume much more of the world's resources than those in poorer nations.

Consuming less protects the environment. When we use fewer goods, we put less demand on the earth's scarce resources. However, lowering consumption would probably reduce our standard of living and cause our economy to suffer.

Contaminate/Contaminant

To contaminate means to make something impure, to add something that spoils the original material. The substance that spoils the pure material is called a contaminant. For example, a water supply may be contaminated by germs or by chemicals leaking from a landfill.

Contour Farming

Erosion is a problem when farmers plant crops on hilly land. Contour farming helps reduce that problem. Instead of plowing and planting rows up and down a hill, farmers plant their crops across the side of the hill—along its contours.

Imagine what would happen if farmers planted their rows of plants up and down a hill. When it rained, the rainwater would pour down between the rows, creating gulleys and washing the topsoil down with it. But with contour farming, rainwater must run across the rows as it runs downhill. The roots of the crops slow the water so it carries away much less soil.

Contour farming reduces soil erosion on this farm in the Midwest.

53

Coral Reef

A reef is a rocky underwater structure. Coral reefs are built up by the actions of millions of tiny coral animals. Coral animals, called polyps, are related to sea anemones and jellyfish. They live in colonies in warm tropical oceans. Each coral polyp fastens itself to a hard surface, usually the remains of other coral. Then it produces a hard limestone cup to live in. When it dies, the polyp leaves a little more limestone added to the reef.

Coral animals have a kind of algae that grows within their bodies. The algae provides some of the coral's nutrients. Below a certain depth in the sea, there is not enough light to support the growth of the algae. Therefore, coral lives only in shallow waters.

Crop Rotation

Crop rotation is a widely used farming method. It preserves plant nutrients in the soil and results in better crops.

Every plant needs certain nutrients to grow. If a farmer plants the same crop in a field year after year, the nutrients for that crop are soon used up. Then crop yields become poor. To prevent this, modern farmers rotate crops. A common rotation is to plant corn one year, then wheat or soybeans the next. Corn uses lots of nitrogen to grow. Bacteria on the soybeans' roots replenish the nitrogen in the soil. Often farmers will let a field lie fallow (with no crop) in the third year. Plowing the grasses and weeds into the soil before the next planting also enriches the soil.

Cycle

A cycle is any set of events that repeat themselves.

The natural world has many cycles. Life itself is a cycle of birth, growth, reproduction, and death, repeated generation after generation.

The food webs in any ecosystem are also cycles. Nutrients pass through the system as one living thing eats another. Eventually those nutrients are recycled, when animal droppings enrich the soil and when plants and animals die and decompose.

Many materials are cycled through the environment. They are used and reused, again and again. Nutrients such as nitrogen and phosphorus go through such cycles. So do other materials necessary for life, such as oxygen, carbon, and water (*see* CARBON CYCLE, LIFE CYCLE, NITROGEN CYCLE, PHOSPHORUS CYCLE, WATER CYCLE).

D

Darwin, Charles

Charles Darwin (1809–1882) was a British biologist who wrote *The Origin of Species*. In that book, published in 1859, Darwin explained how species develop and change. His explanation, called the theory of evolution, is the most important idea in biology. Another naturalist, Alfred Russel Wallace, developed the same idea at about the same time.

Darwin created his theory after a 5-year sea voyage that started in 1831. Darwin was ship's naturalist on the HMS *Beagle*, a British survey ship that sailed around South America. Darwin studied the unusual animals on the isolated Galápagos Islands, off the coast of Ecuador. He realized that species develop as each kind of animal gradually adapts to the special conditions of its habitat. Darwin thought and wrote for more than 20 years before finally publishing his ideas in his most famous book.

In addition to the theory of evolution, Darwin is known for his study of earthworms, coral atolls, and many other biological subjects (*see* EVOLUTION, NATURAL SELECTION).

DDT (Dichloro-Diphenyl-Trichloroethane)

DDT is a chemical first synthesized in 1874; its value as an insecticide was discovered by Swiss scientists in 1939. It was used widely in the United States until 1972. DDT was used to kill farm and garden pests, malaria-carrying mosquitoes, lice, and fleas. One reason that DDT was so effective is that it is long-lasting; it kept killing insects for an extended period of time.

In the 1960s scientists discovered that DDT stays in the food chain, stored in the body fat of animals.

Birds, amphibians, and small mammals died when they ate insects or other smaller animals contaminated with the poison. Birds with DDT in their bodies also laid thin-shelled eggs that broke before they could hatch. Predatory birds like eagles, hawks, and pelicans were dying off. Traces of DDT were also found in human milk.

In 1972 the use of DDT was strictly limited in the United States. Since then, populations of some of the affected birds have started to recover. However, traces of DDT still linger in the environment. And despite its dangers, DDT is still used for mosquito control in other countries.

Death Rate

The death rate measures the number of deaths in a given year for every 1,000 people. The death rate in the United States, for example, is about 8.7 deaths per 1,000 people each year.

When the death rate of a population is lower than the birthrate, the population increases. The world's human population is currently growing at a rate of 1.7 percent per year. Our death rate is much lower than our birthrate. Better food supplies and medical care have helped lower the death rate in the past hundred years (*see* BIRTHRATE).

Decomposers

Decomposers are organisms that digest and break down dead animals and plants. They include bacteria, fungi, and maggots (fly larvae). Decomposers are an important part of the food web. Without them, dead plants and animals would build up rapidly in the environment. Decomposers return to the soil the nutrients that plants and animals have absorbed. That enriches the soil so that new plants and animals can grow.

Demographics

Demographics is the study of human populations. A demographer studies such things as age, gender, birthrates, geographical distribution, and migrations of people. A census is the most important tool of demographics.

Demographers look for patterns and changes in human population. For example, one of the biggest demographic changes in the United States over the past 200 years is the move to the cities. In 1800, about 5 percent of the U.S. population lived in cities. In 1900, well over 50 percent of the people still lived in the countryside. But by 1990, about 75 percent of U.S. residents lived in urban areas.

Department of Energy

The Department of Energy is the federal department responsible for overseeing U.S. energy policy. It regulates interstate commerce in electrical power, coal, oil and gas, and plans for the nation's future energy needs. The department is also responsible for the production of nuclear weapons and the regulation of nuclear power plants. A small percentage of the department's budget goes toward the development of alternative energy sources.

The Department of Energy was established in 1977, during the Carter administration. The Secretary of Energy is a member of the president's cabinet.

Desert

Desert is land that has very little rainfall—10 inches or less per year. The desert is one of earth's major biomes. There are large areas of desert in North and South America, Asia, Africa, and Australia.

Deserts are not necessarily hot, although many, like the Sahara and Mojave deserts, are. The Gobi Desert in Asia is an example of a cold desert. Much of Antarctica is also considered a desert.

Because rainfall is both rare and unpredictable in deserts, these regions are not biologically very productive. The plants and animals living there have adapted to harsh conditions. Many desert plants germinate, bloom, and produce seeds very quickly when there is rain.

Typical plants in the North American desert include a variety of cacti, yucca, creosote bushes, and sagebrush. Animals include snakes and lizards, small rodents, coyotes, foxes, and owls.

Desertification

Desertification is the process by which fertile land turns to desert. Desertification happens naturally, as rainfall patterns change. It is also caused by human actions. Cutting trees and shrubs for firewood removes shade and roots that help soil hold moisture. Overgrazing by livestock has a similar effect. Erosion of plowed farmland also contributes to desertification.

Almost 200,000 square miles of the Sahel, the region south of the Sahara, have become desertified in recent years as a result of human actions and climatic changes. In the 1970s, the Sahara expanded at about 30 miles per year. Desertification is also occurring in other parts of the world. In the United States, Arizona, New Mexico, and parts of the Great Plains are becoming more desertlike.

Detritus

Detritus is the dead, partially decomposed remains

of plants and animals. The layer of dead leaves and twigs on the forest floor is detritus. So is the layer of decomposing plants and animals that settles to the bottom of a lake or bay. As it decomposes, detritus releases nutrients that living plants use. Bacteria, protists (single-celled creatures), and small animals also feed on detritus. In this way, the nutrients in the detritus return to the food chain.

Development (Industrial)

Development is the process by which a country changes from an agricultural economy to an industrial economy. Many of the world's nations—especially in Europe and North America—are already very developed. They use high technology to manufacture the goods and services their citizens rely on. Other developed nations include Japan, Australia, and Argentina.

Other nations—particularly in Africa, Asia, and South America—are still in the early stages of development. Most people in these developing nations live on small farms or make products by hand with simple tools. Many people in developing nations live in poor, overcrowded, and unsanitary conditions.

Development makes life more comfortable. But it is also hard on the environment. Developed nations use large amounts of energy and other resources to keep their factories and transportation systems running. They produce much more waste and pollution. Development also requires people to live close together in cities and live faster-paced lives.

Because the world has limited resources, development, too, must be limited. If we use nonrenewable resources to build an advanced society, we won't be able to sustain it when the resources run out. If we ruin the environment as we develop, we won't have a good quality of life for very long.

"Sustainable development" is the compromise goal of most economic planners. Sustainable development involves becoming a modern, industrialized nation while preserving the resources that make development possible. It is a very difficult goal to achieve.

Development (Urban)

Urban development refers to the process of city building. Development changes farmland or forest or prairie into homes, shopping centers, businesses, and roads. It also destroys natural habitats for wildlife and takes agricultural land out of use.

Much of the development of the United States took place with little planning. People simply bought land and developed it as they chose. In recent years, however, more planning has been required. Land is zoned for certain uses—homes, factories, businesses, or farms. In addition, developers must file environmental impact statements, after studying the possible effects of the development, before they start building.

Every town and city has a strong reason to allow more development: Developed land produces more economic benefits—income and tax revenue—than woodland or farmland. But with each new development, more of the natural environment is lost.

Diatom

Diatoms are single-celled creatures, members of the kingdom Protista. They live in huge numbers near the surface of the world's oceans and fresh waters, where there's plenty of light. Diatoms are sometimes considered a kind of algae. They contain chlo-

61

rophyll. Like plants, they use sunlight and carbon dioxide to produce their own food.

Diatoms and other single-celled plantlike organisms are the base of the aquatic food chain. They provide food for tiny planktonic animals that are, in turn, food for larger species. Diatoms also produce oxygen in the process of photosynthesis (*see* PHYTOPLANKTON).

Dioxins

Dioxins are a group of complex chemicals. They are thought to be among the most toxic synthetic substances on earth. Dioxins cause severe skin rash, headache, and intestinal problems. They are also thought to cause cancer and birth defects. But scientists don't yet agree about the danger of these chemicals. There have been no known deaths directly caused by dioxin poisoning.

Dioxins are not used in industry. They are made in small amounts as a by-product when factories produce herbicides. They are also waste products of other industrial processes.

Dioxins were found in Agent Orange, a herbicide used by U.S. forces in the Vietnam War. Veterans had many health problems after being exposed to Agent Orange. In 1983, the town of Times Beach, Missouri, was evacuated after oil contaminated with dioxins was spread on the roads (*see* AGENT ORANGE, TIMES BEACH).

Dissolved Oxygen

Small amounts of oxygen and other gases can dissolve in water. Plants and animals that live in water need this oxygen for respiration (breathing). Fish, for example, absorb the dissolved oxygen through their gills. If the amount of dissolved oxygen is too low, animals will die.

The amount of oxygen dissolved in water depends on:

- Water temperature. Cool water holds more dissolved gas than warm water. The higher the temperature of a pond or lake, the less oxygen it can hold.

- Water motion. Breaking waves or the swirling water in river rapids or waterfalls mixes air into the water. This mixing helps more oxygen dissolve.

- Concentration of organisms. When large numbers of animals live in a body of water, they use up much of the oxygen. On the other hand, green plants produce more oxygen than they use. Water plants can increase the amount of oxygen in the water.

- Amount of decaying material. Bacteria that digest decaying plant and animal matter use oxygen. Water that has a lot of dead plants and animals in it will have less dissolved oxygen. A sudden die-off of creatures can quickly use up the oxygen in a pond or lake.

Measuring dissolved oxygen is one way of telling how healthy a body of water is. A high level of dissolved oxygen indicates that a pond or stream is a good place for plant and animal life.

Diversity, Biological

Diversity means variety, and biological diversity refers to the number of different species in an ecosystem. Biologists have identified about 1.5 million distinct species of living things on earth. They estimate that another million or more species are yet to be found.

Species are not distributed equally in all habitats. Some ecosystems have many more species than others. In general, regions with warm, moist climates have the greatest biological diversity. The tropical rain forest is the world's most diverse ecosystem. The variety of rain-forest insects and other animals is enormous. Most of the world's undiscovered species live in the tropical rain forest. A five-acre plot of rain forest may contain more than 100 species of trees. Five acres of temperate forest have fewer than 25 species. The northern forests of the taiga have only two dominant tree species, spruce and fir.

DNA (Deoxyribonucleic Acid)

DNA is a large, complicated molecule that carries genetic information in a chemical code. This information tells an organism how to grow and develop. All inherited characteristics of a creature—its heredity—are recorded in its DNA.

There is DNA in the nucleus of each cell in an organism. When organisms reproduce, a copy of their DNA is passed on to their offspring.

Dolphin (*see* MARINE MAMMAL)

Domestication

Domestication is the process of "taming" wild plants or animals for human use. The ancestors of cattle, sheep, and pigs were wild animals. Long ago, humans captured these creatures and learned to tend and care for them. Over many generations, farmers chose the gentlest, most productive animals to breed.

The domesticated animals gradually became better suited for human use. They also became more and more different from their wild relatives.

Farm plants are also domesticated. The ancestors of wheat, corn, and other grains were wild grasses. Farmers selected the best seeds to grow the next year's crops. Their plants grew faster and produced larger harvests. After many generations, domesticated crops are now very different from their wild ancestors. Once a species is domesticated, it may be unable to survive without human care.

Dominant Species

The most common and broadly distributed kinds of plants and animals in an ecosystem are considered its dominant species. For example, the dominant species in the Chesapeake Bay include blue crabs, menhaden, bluefish, oysters, ribbed mussels, eelgrass, and marsh cordgrass. Dominant species in the temperate deciduous forests of North America include oak, maple, hickory, and beech trees, and white-tailed deer, gray squirrels, raccoons, and bobcats.

Dominant species play a central part in the life cycles of an ecosystem. No ecosystem has just a single dominant species.

Dredging

Waterways gradually fill in with mud and silt. Dredging is digging a channel or deepening the bottom of a lake, river, or bay to remove this material. Because of dredging, ships that would otherwise be too large can use a waterway. Dredging may be used to drain a wetland or deepen a lake or pond that has filled in with mud and plants.

Dredging is always a temporary solution. The

processes that fill a river or lake with silt and plants continue after the dredging. Dredging also disturbs the environment. Dredging stirs up the mud that has settled to the bottom of a waterway. If the mud contains harmful chemicals, dredging puts them back into the environment. Dredging wetlands destroys a valuable natural resource.

Dredging also refers to a method of gathering shellfish. This kind of dredge is a heavy basket with rakelike prongs at its open end. A boat drags the dredge across the muddy bottom of an estuary, gathering clams or oysters as it gouges across the bottom. Dredging disturbs the bottom of an estuary and is often limited by fishing regulations.

Drift Net

A drift net is a very long net that commercial fishermen use in the open ocean. Drift nets can be 40 miles long. The top of the net is held at the surface with floats. The bottom is weighted so it hangs down vertically. Fish and other sea creatures swimming past become entangled in the net.

Drift-net fishing is a very effective way to catch fish. But drift nets catch anything that swims into them. Sharks, dolphins, sea turtles, and other creatures die in the net along with the fish that the fishermen want to harvest. This is wasteful and destructive and may put entire species in danger. For that reason, there have been protests in recent years against countries like Japan, whose fleets use drift nets. In 1992 a United Nations resolution banned drift-net fishing.

Drought

A drought is a shortage of rainfall and water supplies. Droughts occur as part of the world's natural weather cycles. Droughts may also occur due to human activity (*see* DESERTIFICATION). A drought may last for a single season or for several years.

When people have little or no extra food and few resources, droughts can cause terrible famines and many deaths. Such disasters have become a frequent event in parts of Africa.

Dump

A dump is a place where trash and garbage are disposed of. Unlike a landfill, trash in a dump is not carefully contained and covered. In most cases, dumps are no longer legal places for disposing of solid wastes (*see* LANDFILL).

Dust Bowl

In the 1930s, a large region of the central United States, including Oklahoma and nearby states, suffered a long drought. The area where this drought occurred became known as the dust bowl. Crops grew poorly without the rain they needed. Because there were few plants to hold the soil in place where farmers had plowed the land, winds blew much of the dry, dusty topsoil away. Many farmers had to leave their lands and move to other parts of the country. Many of these migrants moved to California, where they were known as Okies.

E

Earth Day

Earth Day is an event that reminds us of the importance of caring for our environment. In the late 1960s, more and more citizens became aware of the world's environmental problems.

The first Earth Day was held on April 22, 1970. It included educational events and large political demonstrations around the United States. Since then, other Earth Day celebrations have been held around the United States and in other countries of the world. In some communities, Earth Day has become a yearly event.

Ecological Equivalents

Ecological equivalents are animals or plants from different parts of the world that live in similar environments and have evolved similar adaptations.

For example, bison are large grazing animals that evolved to live in herds on the grasslands of North America. There are no bison in Africa. But the wildebeest is an ecological equivalent—a large animal that grazes in herds on the African grassland. The African ostrich, Australian emu, and South American rhea are also ecological equivalents. All are large, flightless birds adapted to living on the open grassland, with long, powerful legs that help them outrun their predators.

Ecological Succession (*see* SUCCESSION)

Ecology

Ecology is the science that studies relationships between living things and their environment. Ecology is a branch of biology.

Ecosystem

An ecosystem is a group of plants and animals living together in an environment. It also includes all the nonliving physical factors that support them, such as sunlight, water, and minerals. Most of the resources in an ecosystem are continuously recycled, providing food and energy for the organisms living in it.

Ecotone

An ecotone is a border area between two different ecosystems or biomes. The narrow strip of land where a meadow borders a woodland is an ecotone. So is a beach, or the shoreline of a lake.

Many animals use ecotones to hunt, reproduce, or seek shelter. For example, a raccoon may live hidden in a wooded area, but may cross an ecotone to the edge of a pond to hunt for food. Sea turtles cross the ecotone between ocean and land environments to lay their eggs on the beach above the high-tide line.

Effluent

Liquid or gas flowing out from any source is called effluent. Effluent usually refers to waste liquids flowing from a pipe, or the gases coming from a smokestack or exhaust pipe. For example, the wastewater a factory produces is its effluent.

A major cause of water pollution is the effluent, or waste liquids, produced by industry.

Electromagnetic Radiation (*see* IONIZING RADIATION, MICROWAVE RADIATION, SOLAR ENERGY, ULTRAVIOLET RADIATION)

Electrostatic Precipitator

An electrostatic precipitator is a device that reduces the pollution from smokestacks. It removes small particles from the smoke.

Opposite electrical charges attract. An electrostatic precipitator gives the tiny smoke particles an electrical charge. The charged particles are then collected on filters that have the opposite charge.

Endangered Species

An endangered species is a type of plant or animal in danger of extinction. There are so few individuals of the species left that they have difficulty reproducing enough offspring to maintain their population. The world's endangered species include blue whales, rhinoceroses, tigers, snow leopards, gorillas, California condors, whooping cranes, and manatees. Thousands of other lesser-known species are also endangered.

Species become endangered for a number of reasons. They may be overhunted or their habitat may be destroyed by human development. Some species may compete more successfully than others for the same resources. Sometimes a newly introduced predator may find a certain species easy prey.

In most countries, once a species is considered endangered, it is protected by law. Sometimes this protection helps a species survive. Scientists may try to breed endangered animals in captivity and then return them to the wild when their numbers increase. Such captive breeding programs have been tried with a number of species, including California condors, the black-footed ferret, and peregrine falcons.

In the United States, peregrine falcons and brown pelicans have made strong comebacks since being declared endangered. Other species have been less fortunate. There are just a very few California condors left, despite the protection of the Endangered Species Act and the efforts of biologists to breed them in captivity.

A species may become endangered without scientists even being aware of the problem. This is especially true in remote areas like tropical rain forests. A species may even become extinct before anyone realizes that it exists.

Endangered Species Act

The U.S. Congress passed the Endangered Species Act in 1966. Since then, the law has been expanded and strengthened several times. The Endangered Species Act requires the U.S. government to protect plants and animals that are in danger of becoming extinct.

The U.S. secretaries of commerce and the interior decide which species are endangered. About 1,000 species had been placed on the endangered list by the early 1990s. More than 500 of these were in countries other than the United States. Many more species are actually endangered and could be added to the list. Plants and invertebrate species often get less attention than birds, reptiles, and mammals. There are also species threatened with extinction that scientists don't even know about yet.

The Fish and Wildlife Service (part of the Department of the Interior) is responsible for preserving habitat for endangered species. The Commerce Department forbids trade in products made from endangered species, such as ivory from elephant tusks.

Most of the world's nations have joined the effort to protect endangered species through a treaty called the Convention on International Trade in Endangered Species (*see* CITES).

Energy

Energy is the ability to do work. It comes in many forms, including heat, light, electrical energy, chemical energy, and kinetic energy (the energy of motion). Energy can be changed from one form to another. For example, the chemical energy in gasoline is changed to heat when the fuel burns. A gasoline engine then changes some of that heat into motion as it powers a car or truck.

Organisms need energy to live. They use energy to move, grow, stay warm, and reproduce. Plants absorb solar energy and change it to the chemical energy stored in sugars and starches. Animals get energy from the food they eat. Some animals also absorb some energy by basking in the sun.

The word *energy* also refers to the natural resources humans use for heat and power. Petroleum, coal, sunlight, wind power, hydroelectric power, nuclear energy, and geothermal energy are all resources that people use to run machinery and heat buildings.

Energy Crisis

Humans rely on fuel for transportation, heating, and agriculture. When there is a shortage, people suffer, and the economy suffers as well. An energy crisis is a damaging or disastrous shortage of fuels.

The United States experienced an energy crisis in 1973. Oil-producing nations sold less petroleum and raised prices. There were long lines at gasoline stations, shortages of heating oil, and large price increases. The government prepared to ration gasoline and started research to create alternative fuels. People were asked to drive less and turn down their thermostats. The crisis ended as oil producers began selling more petroleum to make more money.

Despite the crisis of 1973, the United States is more dependent on other countries for its energy now than it was 20 years ago. In 1973, the United States imported about 35 percent of the petroleum it used. By 1990, 42 percent of the petroleum used in the United States came from other countries.

The 1973 oil shortage was temporary. But people are facing a serious, long-term energy problem. We have used up most of the earth's supplies of petroleum, coal, and natural gas. At the current rate of use, there are only about 40 to 50 more years of petroleum and 200 more years of coal left in the world's known reserves. That's why conserving energy resources and finding renewable energy sources is so important.

73

Energy Efficiency

Energy efficiency means getting the most use from an energy resource. For example, the more miles per gallon of gasoline a car gets, the more energy-efficient it is.

Some forms of transportation are more energy-efficient than others. Trains and ships can carry large amounts of cargo and large numbers of people. They use fuel more efficiently than buses and trucks. Buses and trucks are, in turn, more efficient than passenger cars. Car pooling improves the efficiency of an automobile, of course, because it uses the same amount of energy to carry more passengers. Bicycles are the most energy-efficient form of transportation.

Appliances such as refrigerators, water heaters, freezers, and air conditioners use large amounts of electrical energy. In stores, these appliances have yellow EnergyGuide tags that rate their efficiency. The tags let consumers compare the energy efficiency of different brands of appliances and make wise buying decisions.

People can improve the energy efficiency of their homes in many ways. These include installing insulation and storm windows, lowering the thermostat on furnaces and water heaters, and turning off unused lights and appliances. Because electricity and fuels are expensive, factories and businesses try to use energy more efficiently, too. Cogeneration is one way that factories can improve their energy efficiency (*see* COGENERATION).

Environment

Environment means surroundings. A creature's environment includes all the plants and animals that live around it. Its environment also includes abiotic (nonliving) factors like the landscape, sunlight, and climate.

74

Environmental Impact Statement

An environmental impact statement (EIS) is a report required by federal law whenever a private company or government agency plans a large construction project. The law requiring such reports took effect in 1970.

Planners of construction projects such as dams, power plants, factories, airports, and large residential and commercial developments must file environmental impact statements. The report must be approved before building can begin. The EIS analyzes what damage the project would do to the environment. The planners must also consider alternatives to their project, to see if another method might do less damage.

Groups that oppose a project often use environmental impact statements as evidence when they try to stop a development.

Environmental Injustice/Environmental Racism

Waste dumps, polluting industries, incinerators, and other environmentally hazardous projects have often been located in areas where the population is poor and politically less powerful. Racial and ethnic minorities often live in such areas. This practice has come to be called environmental injustice or environmental racism by many ecological activists.

Ecologically damaging projects are often located in these areas because the residents need jobs and because they don't have the political clout to fight the government or business leaders promoting the projects. Unfortunately, polluting projects that provide jobs for residents may also cause serious health problems many years later.

Another example of environmental injustice is the shipping of hazardous wastes from wealthier

75

nations to poorer, less developed ones. Most developing nations don't have the kind of environmental safeguards that rich nations do. The poorer nations need the income that waste disposal generates, but such projects may also create health problems for their own people in the future.

Environmental Protection Agency (EPA)

The Environmental Protection Agency was established in 1970. The EPA is responsible for safeguarding the environment in our country. It does research and sets environmental standards and policies. It is also responsible for enforcing the nation's environmental laws and regulations.

The EPA is currently an independent agency of the federal government. The director of the EPA is a member of the president's cabinet. In 1993, President Bill Clinton proposed that the EPA become the Department of the Environment.

Epidemic

An epidemic is a widespread outbreak of disease. Epidemics are more common when an animal or plant species has become overpopulated. In that situation, individuals are weaker because there is not enough food. Disease spreads more easily because individuals are in close contact with one another.

Epidemics can serve a positive purpose for an ecosystem. Although it kills many individuals, an epidemic may eliminate overcrowding and help a species maintain a strong, stable population.

Erosion

Erosion is the wearing away of the land by running

water, waves, wind, or ice. Erosion can be very destructive—as when heavy rains or dust storms carry soil away from a farmer's fields.

Erosion also builds new land, when the particles that have been carried away are finally deposited somewhere else. The earth's soil is made from tiny particles of rock and sand that have been eroded from ancient mountains. The Mississippi Delta, a very fertile area, is built from soil that has been eroded and washed down the Mississippi River.

Erosion is a natural process in any environment, but it is increased by human actions. Plowed land loses much more soil to wind and water erosion than grassland does, where plant roots hold down the soil. And because forested areas slow the flow of rainwater, hillsides that have been cleared of timber often have serious erosion problems. Developed land also absorbs less rainfall, so more water runs off, creating gullies and washing soil into swollen streams and rivers.

Estuary

An estuary is the flooded mouth of a river, where it flows into the ocean. In an estuary, ocean water mixes with the fresh water from the river itself. The Chesapeake Bay is the world's largest estuary. It formed where the Susquehanna River flows into the Atlantic Ocean. Other notable estuaries in the United States include Delaware Bay, Mobile Bay, New York Harbor, and Galveston Bay.

Estuaries are among the most fertile and productive ecosystems on earth. They have everything needed for plant and animal growth. Estuaries are usually shallow, so the sun warms them quickly. Rivers wash lots of nutrients into estuaries. And they are protected from the harsh storms and waves of the open ocean.

Estuaries are breeding grounds and nurseries for oysters, clams, shrimp, crabs, fish, and waterbirds. They are attractive places for people, too. Millions of people live along the shores of the Chesapeake Bay, for example. Estuaries also make safe harbors for ships.

Human activities often threaten the health of estuaries. Pollution from farming (fertilizers and pesticides), lawn care, sewage treatment, automobiles, and other human activities runs into the estuary. Estuaries also get heavy recreational use. Fishing and boating can change the ecological balance of an estuary. Road building and housing developments destroy wildlife habitats. These human activities can make life difficult for other species in the estuary.

A satellite view of Chesapeake Bay, the largest estuary in the world

Eutrophication

Eutrophication is a natural process by which a lake or pond gradually becomes richer in nutrients. Plants and animals grow in and around a pond. As they die and decay, they provide nutrients for further plant and animal growth. The pond becomes more productive and full of life.

Over many years, as eutrophication continues, a pond or lake fills in with biological material. If left alone, the pond eventually becomes a bog or marsh, later a meadowland, and finally a woodland.

Fertilizers that wash into ponds from lawns and farms speed up the process of eutrophication. So do the nutrients from sewage wastes.

Evaporation

Evaporation is the change from a liquid to a gas. It takes energy for this change to occur. As water evaporates, it absorbs large amounts of energy. That's why perspiration cools the skin. As the sweat evaporates, it carries away body heat.

Almost one fourth of the solar energy that reaches the earth goes toward evaporating water from the world's oceans, lakes, and rivers. This energy is carried away by the water vapor in our atmosphere. Later, when the water vapor condenses into clouds and rain, the energy is released in the form of wind and storms.

When water evaporates, it leaves behind the chemical salts and other solids dissolved in it. When farmlands are irrigated in arid regions, the salts are left behind as the water evaporates. The salts can gradually build up in the soil, slowly ruining the land for plant growth. Some chemical salts, especially selenium salts in the western United States, can reach toxic levels. Animals that drink water

79

contaminated with these chemicals, or eat plants that have absorbed them, are then poisoned (*see* SALINATION).

Evolution

Evolution is the process by which species develop and change. According to the theory proposed by Charles Darwin in 1859, evolution works by a process of natural selection. Members of a species have slight differences. Those that are best adapted to their environment are the ones most likely to survive. This is known as survival of the fittest. Individuals that survive longest are most likely to have offspring and pass their adaptations on to them. In this way, over many generations, a species may change and even evolve into new and different species.

The process of evolution is hard to imagine, unless you remember that it usually takes place over a long period of time, sometimes thousands or even millions of years. A lot of small changes, generation by generation, can add up to enormous differences over time (*see* DARWIN, CHARLES *and* NATURAL SELECTION).

Exotic Species

Exotic species are creatures from other environments that have been introduced into an ecosystem, often by humans. As people travel around the world, other species of plants and animals travel with them. We bring some species with us on purpose, like food crops and pets. Others (insects or rats, for example) are hitchhikers—they're transported accidentally. Exotics may also be called introduced species.

When an exotic species settles in a new environment, it competes with the native, or original, species living there. Many familiar plants and animals in the United States that we might think are natives are actually successful exotics. Starlings, sparrows, rats, Japanese beetles, honeysuckle, and apples are just a few examples.

Sometimes exotics compete so well that they eliminate a native species. For example, the native flightless birds on some Pacific islands, such as the kiwi and kakapo of New Zealand, are near extinction because they have no defenses against the cats, dogs, and rats that human settlers brought with them.

Other exotics may cause great damage because there are no natural predators in the new environment to control them. The gypsy moth—an exotic from Europe—has damaged huge areas of American woodlands. It has no natural enemies in North America. Zebra mussels were probably brought to the Great Lakes in ships from Europe. They, too, have no natural predators in America. Zebra mussels have spread throughout the Great Lakes. As they multiply, they clog water pipes and foul the bottoms of ships, causing billions of dollars of damage. They now eat so much of the plankton in the lakes that fish are being deprived of food (*see* NATIVE SPECIES, NATURALIZED SPECIES).

Exponential Growth

Exponential growth is growth at an increasingly fast rate. Industrial and economic development on our planet has grown in this way for many years. The world's economy has been growing at an average rate of about 3.5 percent. This means that each year we produce as much as the year before, *plus* an extra 3.5 percent. This might not seem like much, but it means that every 20 years, production doubles.

More growth might seem to be a good thing. But earth's resources are limited. There aren't enough minerals, fuels, and other raw materials to maintain this growth forever. At this rate of exponential growth, resources will run out. When that happens, industrial production will drop suddenly.

Somehow people must control industrial and economic growth to preserve the world's resources. At the same time, we must try to maintain a decent standard of living for the world's growing population. It will not be an easy task, if it is possible at all.

Extinction

Extinction is the dying out of a species. It may take place when the environment changes so much that a species can't successfully adapt to the change. For example, a rapid change of climate might destroy a species. Scientists think that such a climatic change might have led to the extinction of the dinosaurs.

Extinction can also happen when a species loses its habitat, or a new kind of plant or animal overwhelms it and hunts or crowds it out of existence. For example, billions of passenger pigeons once lived in eastern North America. But hunters managed to destroy the entire species. The last passenger pigeon died in 1914. Flightless birds like the dodo of Mauritius, an island in the Indian Ocean, and the moa of New Zealand were killed off by a combination of human hunters and predators such as pigs, rats, and dogs introduced into their environments.

Exxon Valdez (*see* OIL SPILL)

Fallout

Fallout is the radioactive dust that settles to the earth after a nuclear accident or explosion. Fallout can cause radiation poisoning, burns, and cancer.

The United States developed the first atomic bombs and dropped them on the Japanese cities of Hiroshima and Nagasaki in 1945. From 1945 until the early 1960s, the United States and the Soviet Union exploded hundreds of nuclear weapons in above-ground tests. Fallout spread around the world. It entered the food chain. Farm animals ate contaminated grass and grain. When radioactivity was found in the baby teeth of children, people around the world insisted that the testing be stopped. In 1963, the two countries agreed to limit themselves to underground nuclear tests. Since then, radiation levels from fallout have dropped steadily.

Accidents at nuclear power plants, including Chernobyl and Three Mile Island, have also produced radioactive fallout that has been detected around the world.

Famine

Famine is widespread starvation. A famine may have many different causes. It's most likely to occur where people are already living with very few resources. Overpopulation also makes famine more likely. Those who are weak and powerless, usually children and the elderly, suffer the most in time of famine.

Natural disasters such as droughts, floods, or other climatic changes can cause food shortages that lead to famine. Famine is also a result of war. When combat interrupts transportation and trade, people may not be able to get the food they need. Many of the worst famines of this century have occurred during wartime.

FDA (*see* FOOD AND DRUG ADMINISTRATION)

Federal Water Pollution Control Act (Clean Water Act)

The Federal Water Pollution Control Act was first passed in 1948. It has been strengthened several times since then. This U.S. law sets rules and standards for sewage treatment and other discharges into streams, lakes, and rivers.

Through the law the U.S. Congress gives money to cities and towns that need to build or improve sewage treatment plants. Thanks in part to this law, 75 percent of U.S. waterways have improved in quality since 1972. Unfortunately, some communities still have not received funding to enable them to build sewage treatment plants that meet the law's clean water standards.

Fertilizer

Fertilizer is any material that adds plant nutrients to the soil. The three main nutrients in fertilizers are nitrogen, phosphorus, and potassium. Commercial fertilizer is labeled with three numbers. They show the amount of each of these nutrients it contains. For example, 5-10-5 fertilizer is 5 percent nitrogen, 10 percent phosphorus, and 5 percent potassium.

Some farmers use organic materials such as manure, bonemeal, and wood ashes as sources for plant nutrients. Most, however, use fertilizers made artificially by chemical companies. Nitrogen fertilizer can be made from natural gas and nitrogen from the air. Potassium chloride and phosphate rock are obtained from mineral deposits. Fertilizers are also made from slaughterhouse wastes, treated sewage, and guano (bird and bat droppings).

Fertilizers cause pollution when they run off into lakes or rivers. There they cause rapid algae growth. When the algae run out of nutrients, they die. The water's oxygen becomes used up as the algae decompose, causing other plants and animals to die.

Fire

Fire, started by lightning strikes, is a natural factor in many ecosystems. Fire clears away dead and dying plants and opens areas for new plants to sprout and grow. Some plants, like lodgepole pine, need the heat of a fire to release their seeds.

Human efforts to control forest fires, brushfires, and prairie fires may cause more harm than good. When fires are prevented for many years, large amounts of dry wood and brush build up. Then, when a fire finally does start, it is more destructive and harder to control.

In the United States, there has been debate about whether fires in national parks and wilderness areas should be allowed to burn. Currently, fires set by humans are put out, but naturally started fires are allowed to burn —as long as they don't threaten human settlements.

Fish Kill

When some factor in a river, lake, or ocean goes out of balance, fish and other water animals can be killed. There are many reasons for fish kills, both natural and human-made. Fish may be killed by rapid temperature changes, toxic leaks, red tides (caused by toxic algae blooms), loss of oxygen in the water, acid rain, or other causes. A fish kill is easy to see, so it can serve as a signal that something has gone wrong in an ecosystem.

Floodplain

A floodplain is a low-lying area of land that can be flooded by rains, overflowing rivers, or ocean storms. Because the floodwaters bring soil and nutrients, floodplains are usually very fertile farmland.

People living on floodplains risk losing their homes and lives. In the United States, many communities have zoning restrictions that prohibit construction of homes or other buildings in areas that are subject to flooding. Nevertheless, many people live in floodplains by choice or by necessity. In 1991, in Bangladesh, 100,000 people died and millions became homeless when a huge storm swept over much of the country's floodplains (*see* BANGLADESH).

Food and Drug Administration (FDA)

The Food and Drug Administration is part of the U.S. Department of Health and Human Services. The FDA's job is to protect the purity of food sold in the United States. The FDA also tries to ensure that drugs and medical devices are safe and effective. It also regulates the proper labeling of foods and medicines and inspects food processing plants and warehouses.

The FDA tests products and sets standards for the purity of foods and medicines. No FDA standard requires a food to be completely free of contamination. For example, fish can contain up to two parts per million of PCBs, a toxic chemical, and still be sold in the market. The FDA tests only a small sample of all the food and medicine sold in the United States.

Food Chain

A food chain is a series of organisms, from green plants to herbivores to carnivores, each of which is eaten by the next creature along the chain. Energy and nutrients are passed from one creature to the next through the food chain.

The diagram that follows shows one simple example of a food chain. At the base of the chain, the leaves and seeds of green plants provide food for chipmunks and other small mammals. The chipmunks are then eaten by a large predator such as a bobcat.

Food Pyramid

All food chains start when plants absorb solar energy and produce food. The energy that nourishes all the creatures in an ecosystem comes from that one source. But not all the energy at one level in the food chain is passed on to the next level. Not all plants and animals get eaten. Enough survive to reproduce. And not all food energy goes to produce new body mass. Some is digested and used to supply energy for life's activities; some food simply passes through the digestive system and is returned to the environment in animal droppings.

To support just a few large predators at the top of the food chain, many more smaller animals are needed. Feeding those smaller animals takes an even larger amount of plants. That's why a food chain is more accurately thought of as a food pyramid.

As a general rule, it takes about 10 pounds of food to produce 1 pound of animal at the next level of the food chain. For example, it would take about 10,000 pounds of algae and other phytoplankton to support 1,000 pounds of copepods, daphnia, and other zooplankton. That much zooplankton could support about 100 pounds of minnows. In turn, those minnows would feed about 10 pounds of bass. And that 10 pounds of bass would be enough for an osprey to gain 1 pound of weight.

Food Web

A food web is a group of interconnected food chains that represents who eats who in an ecosystem.

Few creatures eat only one kind of food. Feeding patterns in an ecosystem can be very complicated.

For example, bass in a pond eat frogs, snakes, smaller fish, insects, crayfish, and even small mammals. Each of these creatures is in turn a part of a different food chain. A food web is an attempt to describe all the different relationships of producers and consumers in an environment.

Forestry

Forestry is the industry of planting, growing, and harvesting trees. Trees provide raw materials for lumber, plywood, paper, fuel, and chemical products such as turpentine, rayon, and cellophane.

Forestry is an important part of the U.S. and world economies. In the United States, forestry and its related industries employ about 1.5 million people and produce $120 billion in paper, fibers, and building materials. Forestry companies own more than 70 million acres of U.S. woodlands. They harvest trees on large areas of public land as well.

Some forestry practices can severely damage the environment. Clear-cutting, or cutting down all the trees in an area, can lead to soil erosion, loss of soil nutrients, water pollution, and the destruction of wildlife habitat (*see* CLEAR-CUTTING, SELECTIVE CUTTING).

Fossil Fuels

Coals, natural gas, and petroleum are fossil fuels. These fuels were formed from the bodies of dead plants and animals. The remains of these organisms have been buried under layers of sedimentary rock for many millions of years. Time and pressure changed these creatures into oil or coal.

Fossil fuels are a nonrenewable resource. The same processes that formed these fuels still occur today. But they happen *very* slowly. Plants that die and fall into a bog today won't become coal for millions of years.

Our modern society relies very heavily on fossil fuels. About 90 percent of the world's energy comes from the burning of coal, petroleum, and natural gas. In addition to providing energy, fossil fuels are used to make medicines, fabrics, fertilizers, plastics, and thousands of other products. Because of these many other uses, they could even be thought of as too valuable to burn.

Meanwhile, we are using up fossil fuels at a very fast rate. Most of the world's oil will be used up within 40 to 50 years. Natural gas will last only a few years longer. Coal is expected to last about 200 years. In order to sustain our modern society, we will have to find renewable sources of energy to take the place of fossil fuels.

Fungus; Fungi (plural)

Fungi are a group of organisms that include molds, mildews, yeasts, and mushrooms. Many types of fungi break down and digest dead plants and animals. As decomposers, fungi play an important part in the web of life. They allow nutrients to be returned to the soil so that they are available to living creatures again. Some fungi, such as corn smut and athlete's foot fungus, live as parasites on other organisms.

Biologists have identified over 100,000 different species of fungi. In the past, fungi have been considered part of the plant kingdom, but most biologists now consider fungi to be a separate and distinct kingdom of organisms. Fungi cannot use sunlight to produce their own food as plants can. The branch of biology that studies fungi is known as mycology.

G

Gasohol

Gasohol is gasoline mixed with about 10 percent alcohol. Gasoline, made from petroleum, is a nonrenewable energy resource. But alcohol is made from grain or wood pulp—it's renewable. Adding alcohol to the gasoline makes the nonrenewable fuel last longer.

Gasohol also burns cleaner in car engines, so that automobiles produce less air pollution.

Gene Pool

Genes are the carriers of heredity. All of a species' genetic information is recorded chemically on the genes in every cell. The gene pool is all the individuals of a species that are able to reproduce and continue the species.

The genes of each individual are slightly different. That's what accounts for our different heights, shapes, eye color, skin color, and all the other individual qualities that we see in people. These variations exist in other creatures as well.

These small differences help a species survive. When the environment changes, variations in the gene pool let a species adapt to those changes. Over time, the individuals with useful variations live and reproduce successfully, and the species adapts to the new conditions.

When the population of a species decreases, the gene pool also becomes small. This makes it harder for the species to adapt. The variations it needs may simply not be found within the gene pool.

91

Individuals' genes also have minor defects. Ordinarily, these are not important. But if the gene pool is too small, it is more likely that the remaining individuals will pass on the defects. That makes it harder for their offspring to survive.

Geothermal Energy

Geothermal energy comes from the heat beneath the earth's crust. In some places, this heat is very near the surface. It creates hot springs, geysers, and even volcanoes.

To tap geothermal energy, pipes are drilled into the hot rock. Water pumped through the pipes boils into steam. The steam is then used to generate electric power or to heat buildings. Iceland has lots of volcanic activity, so it is well supplied with geothermal energy. All the homes in Reykjavík, Iceland's capital, are heated with geothermal energy. In the United States, there is a geothermal energy generating station at The Geysers in northern California.

Geothermal energy causes almost no pollution. But its use is limited to those places where the earth's heat is near the surface.

Global Warming

Since about 1850, the earth's climate has gradually become warmer. Average temperatures have risen about 1°F during this time. This situation is known as global warming.

If the climate warms by only a few more degrees, there will be big environmental changes on our planet. Sea level will rise, flooding coastal cities. There could be more tropical storms and hurricanes. Areas that had enough rainfall could become deserts, while some dry areas might become lush and fertile.

And there would be big changes in living conditions for humans, plants, and animals. Some scientists predict that the earth's average temperature could rise as much as seven to nine degrees by the year 2100. However, accurate predictions are difficult because so many different factors affect the world's climate.

No one knows how serious a problem global warming is, or how fast it is happening. Weather patterns are always variable. It's impossible to tell whether any one day or season or year is warmer than average because of global warming. An unusually warm period could just be a result of chance weather variations. However, the evidence seems to show that our climate is getting warmer. The eight warmest years of the 20th century have all come since 1979.

What causes global warming? The earth's climate naturally goes through long cycles of warmer and cooler temperatures. There were at least four ice ages (global cooling) in our planet's distant history. Each ice age was followed by a long warmer period. It's possible the earth may now be experiencing a similar "warm age." But many scientists believe that the main cause is a buildup of greenhouse gases in the atmosphere. These gases, including carbon dioxide, CFCs, and methane, are produced by human activity (*see* GREENHOUSE EFFECT).

The world's governments are trying to agree on limiting greenhouse gas emissions. And every person can also help reduce greenhouse gases by planting trees, consuming less, driving less, and using energy-efficient appliances.

Grassland

Grassland is one of the earth's major biomes. In the United States, grasslands are known as the prairie.

The prairie extends from Indiana and Illinois to Wyoming and Colorado, from the Dakotas to Texas. In South America, grasslands are called the pampas. In Eurasia, they're called the steppes, and in Africa, the veld.

Grasslands are flat or gently rolling areas in the earth's temperate regions. They're covered with grasses and other low-growing plants. Grasslands have limited rainfall—from 10 to 30 inches per year—with hot, dry summers and cool or cold winters. North American grassland animals include bison, deer, prairie dogs, rabbits, and birds such as grouse and prairie chickens, ducks, and geese.

Gray Water

Gray water is the wastewater from washing. It comes from sinks, tubs, washing machines, and dishwashers. Gray water is easier to treat than wastewater from toilets, which contains human wastes. In some home septic systems, gray water is treated separately from sewage wastes.

Greenbelt

A greenbelt is a planned region of trees and parkland surrounding or running through a city or town. Planners include greenbelts in their designs for a city's growth. Greenbelts beautify a city and make life there more pleasant. Trees provide cooling shade and add oxygen to the air. And the parkland provides recreation areas for city residents.

Greenhouse Effect

A greenhouse is a glass building used to grow plants indoors. Sunlight shines through the glass windows and warms the inside of the building. The windows keep the heat from escaping back outside. The greenhouse stays much warmer than the outside air.

Carbon dioxide, water vapor, and other gases in the earth's atmosphere act much like the windows of a greenhouse. Sunlight shines through the atmosphere, warming the planet. Most of that heat is then radiated back out into space. But the greenhouse gases trap some of that heat and prevent it from leaving the atmosphere. So the earth gradually becomes warmer (*see* GLOBAL WARMING).

The gas most responsible for the greenhouse effect is carbon dioxide (CO_2). CO_2 is produced when fuels such as coal, wood, or gasoline are burned. Because we depend on these fuels for so much of our energy, we produce huge amounts of carbon dioxide every day.

Green plants absorb carbon dioxide from the atmosphere, in the process of photosynthesis. But plants can't absorb as much CO_2 as we produce. So the amount of carbon dioxide in the atmosphere has gradually been increasing.

The United States is the world's largest producer of CO_2. Even though we have only 5 percent of the world's population, U.S. factories, furnaces, and automobiles produce more than 20 percent of the world's CO_2.

Other gases, including methane and CFCs, also trap heat and contribute to the greenhouse effect. Methane is found in natural gas. It is released into the atmosphere when gas wells or pipelines leak. It is also produced in animals' intestines as a by-product of digestion. CFCs (which also destroy ozone) enter the atmosphere from fire extinguishers and leaky refrigerators and air conditioners. Scientists may disagree about the seriousness of the problem, but they believe the increased amount of CO_2 and the other greenhouse gases in the atmosphere is the main cause of global warming.

95

Green Politics

Green politics is the effort to include concern for the environment in the government of states and countries.

Green politics became an important force in Europe in the 1980s. Green parties won seats in the parliaments of many European countries. The Green party was particularly strong in Germany, where it supported nuclear disarmament. Small local green parties have also formed in the United States and elsewhere in the world. Currently, these groups have little influence on government policy.

The term *green politics* also refers to activities within more traditional party politics. Environmental concerns are important to voters. Politicians in the major U.S. political parties often take pro-environmental stands. Organizations like the Sierra Club and Friends of the Earth lobby for laws to protect the environment. These activities can also be called green politics.

Green Revolution

Green revolution is the name given to new agricultural methods that came into use after World War II. These included new chemical fertilizers and pesticides, and more productive varieties of crops such as wheat, rice, and corn. The green revolution helped farmers around the world grow more food. In some developing countries, food production grew faster than the population for the first time. For a few years, it looked as if the green revolution might end world hunger.

But the new methods were not as miraculous as people first thought. Many of them are too expensive for small farmers in the developing world. Some use large amounts of energy, or require special machinery or workers with special training. Insects have become resistant to the new pesticides. Droughts, erosion, and irrigation problems have all made it difficult to keep up the progress of the green revolution. Nevertheless, farmers around the world now produce more food than they did before the green revolution.

Groundwater

Groundwater is the water flowing in aquifers beneath the earth's surface. Rainwater trickles down through the soil to feed the underground pools of groundwater. Groundwater is the source for the water in springs and underground wells (see AQUIFER).

H

Habitat

A habitat is the place where an organism lives. Habitat provides the food, water, and shelter that a creature needs. Both living and nonliving features of the environment are considered part of an organism's habitat.

For example, a fiddler crab's habitat is a salt marsh. The habitat of kelp is cool, coastal ocean waters with rocky bottoms. Some creatures need very specialized habitats in order to survive, while others are able to adapt to a wider range of living conditions.

Hardpan (*see* COMPACTION)

Hazardous Waste

Hazardous waste is any waste material that is dangerous to humans or wildlife. The disposal of hazardous waste is now strictly regulated by the Environmental Protection Agency, but in the past, huge quantities of hazardous waste contaminated many environments. Many hazardous wastes, including household chemicals, are still disposed of illegally despite these rules (*see* MEDICAL WASTES, RADIOACTIVE WASTE, TOXIC WASTE).

Heat Balance/Heat Budget

A heat budget is the balance of all the energy going into and out of an environment. Let's consider the earth's heat budget. The earth receives its heat energy from the sun. About 30 percent is reflected back into space. The rest of it is absorbed by the air, water, and land. The energy that is absorbed by the oceans and atmosphere drives our planet's climate and ocean currents. About 1 to 2 percent of the sun's energy is absorbed by plants in the process of photosynthesis.

There must be a balance between the energy the earth absorbs and the energy it gives off. Eventually, all the solar energy that the earth absorbs is radiated back into space. Otherwise our planet would get hotter and hotter. Because industrial processes have put more carbon dioxide into the atmosphere, this balance has changed slightly in the past two centuries. Earth's temperatures have become slightly warmer (*see* GLOBAL WARMING, GREENHOUSE EFFECT).

Heavy Metals

Heavy metals are chemical elements such as lead, mercury, cadmium, and arsenic. They are called heavy metals because they are generally among the densest, or heaviest, of the chemical elements. These substances have many important industrial and commercial uses. For example, mercury is used in electrical switches, dental fillings, and the refining of other metals. Lead was used for many years in paints, gasoline, printing, and plumbing. These chemicals are also poisonous. When heavy metals get into the air, food, or water supply, they can kill or injure people and animals.

Children are most sensitive to heavy-metal poisoning. Lead poisoning, for example, damages the brain, kidneys, and liver. In children, it causes mental and physical retardation and learning difficulties. Children can get lead poisoning from flaking, peeling paint in older homes, from water in old household plumbing, or even from roadsides contaminated with car exhaust.

Heavy metals bioaccumulate. They stay in the body for long periods of time. Once they get into a food chain, they're passed on from consumer to consumer, getting more and more concentrated. Because they are chemical elements, they can't be broken down into other harmless substances.

One of the worst cases of heavy-metal poisoning occurred in Minamata, Japan. In the 1950s, people and animals in this fishing village began developing headaches, blurred vision, and slurred speech. Some people became paralyzed and died. Children were born with birth defects. Eventually the cause was traced to mercury poisoning. A chemical factory owned by the Chisso Corporation was dumping waste mercury compounds into Minamata Bay. People were poisoned by eating contaminated seafood. It was only after many years of legal disputes that the company was forced to pay damages to some of the victims.

In recent years, more effort has been made to keep heavy metals out of the environment. For example, all gasoline and house paint sold in the United States is now lead-free. Lead pipes have been removed from school buildings, and lead can no longer be used to solder (connect) water pipes.

Herbicide

A herbicide is a chemical that kills plants. Herbicides are most often used by farmers to control weeds. Although they are meant to kill plants, many of these chemicals can also harm people and animals.

Some herbicides, called selective herbicides, kill only certain types of weed plants without killing a desirable crop. Others, called nonselective, kill all plant life. Herbicides that kill weed seeds as they sprout are called preemergent herbicides. Postemergent herbicides are used to kill weeds that are already growing.

Herbivore

A herbivore is an animal that feeds on plants. Cattle, rabbits, beaver, and deer are all examples of herbivores. Herbivores are also known as primary consumers, because they are the first animals in the food chain to consume—or eat—plant products (*see* CARNIVORE, OMNIVORE).

Heredity

Heredity is the process by which plants and animals inherit features from their parents. For example, the color of a girl's eyes or skin is passed to her from her parents through heredity. So are all the other special characteristics that an individual has. Body shape and size, the functions of body organs, and even some instinctive behaviors are passed on through heredity.

Hereditary information is contained in each cell in the body. The information is encoded in a chemical called DNA. DNA makes up the genes and contains all the directions an organism needs to grow and develop. This information is passed on from parent organisms to each new offspring.

Information carried in the genes can change if the chemical makeup of the DNA is changed. These changes, called mutations, may be helpful or harmful. Mutations are also passed on from generation to generation through heredity.

Hiroshima (*see* NUCLEAR WEAPONS)

101

Host (*see* PARASITE)

Humus

Dead leaves, wood, and other plant matter gradually decay into a soft, dark brown material called humus. Humus is an important ingredient of topsoil. Not surprisingly, areas with heavy plant growth, such as forests, have large amounts of humus.

Humus enriches the soil. The rotted material contains nutrients that the plants took from the soil as they grew. Because it is spongy, humus also helps the soil absorb water. There is less runoff and erosion after heavy rains if the soil has plenty of humus.

Hydrocarbons

Hydrocarbons are a large family of chemicals composed of hydrogen and carbon atoms. Petroleum fuels such as gasoline and diesel oil are hydrocarbons. So are animal fats and vegetable oils.

When hydrocarbons burn completely, the result is water vapor and carbon dioxide gas. But incompletely burned fuels in engine exhaust pollute the air with hydrocarbon molecules, as well as carbon monoxide. Cooking meat also produces large amounts of hydrocarbon pollution. Hydrocarbon pollution is one of the main ingredients of smog.

Hydroelectric Power

Hydroelectric power is electricity generated by the force of falling water. To generate electricity, a dam is built. Water from the lake behind the dam pours through turbines—spinning blades that turn electrical generators. The generators change the water power into electrical energy.

Hydroelectric power can be generated on very large scales, such as at the Grand Coulee Dam in Washington State or Hoover Dam in Nevada. Or it can be generated by small dams that produce just enough power for a business or a small community.

Hydroelectric power is one of the cleanest forms of energy. But even hydroelectric power causes environmental damage. A dam floods large areas of land. People may live on that land or value it for its scenic beauty and wildlife habitat. Because of these problems, building a new hydroelectric dam is often a controversial decision.

The Glen Canyon dam and power plant on the Colorado River

Hydrologic Cycle (*see* WATER CYCLE)

Ice Cap

An ice cap is the layer of ice covering the coldest regions of a planet's surface. The earth is covered by ice caps at both the north and south polar regions. Polar ice caps grow larger during winter months and smaller during the summer.

In places, the ice caps have been built up over many thousands of years. Years of snowfall form a thick icy sheet. The Greenland ice cap is more than two miles thick in some places. The Antarctic ice cap is more than three miles thick. In other areas, the ice cap is a sheet of ice only a few feet thick that forms over the polar seas in winter but melts again each summer.

At various times in the past, the ice caps covered much larger areas of the earth's surface than they do today. During those times—known as the ice ages—the earth's climate was much cooler.

Most of the earth's fresh water is frozen in the polar ice caps. One concern people have about global warming is its effect on the ice caps. If the earth's climate gets a few degrees warmer, some of the polar ice caps could melt. That would add water to the oceans, raising the sea level and flooding many coastal areas.

Immobilization (*see* VITRIFICATION)

Incinerator

Incinerate means to burn. An incinerator is a furnace used to burn waste material. Incinerators are used for garbage or trash disposal. When solid waste is incinerated, the ash that remains takes up much less room in a landfill than the solid waste would. However, burning changes the rest of the solid waste to waste gases, producing air pollution. Garbage can also be incinerated to generate energy (*see* BIOMASS).

Incineration is also used to treat medical wastes, because heat destroys disease-causing microbes. Some toxic wastes are also destroyed by incineration.

Indoor Air Pollution

Air pollution can be a problem indoors as well as outside. Usually, tightly sealed modern buildings with windows that don't open have the worst indoor air pollution problems. The pollutants can cause coldlike symptoms or other illnesses. This problem is sometimes called sick building syndrome.

Some building products like paints and glues may give off unpleasant or harmful fumes. Poorly ventilated buildings can also develop mold, which fills the air with irritating spores. Heating systems may not be vented properly. Finding the cause for a sick building problem is often difficult, and solving it can be expensive.

Other causes of indoor air pollution include: smoking, stoves, heaters and fireplaces, asbestos, pesticides, cleaning fluids, and radon gas seeping into the building from the surrounding soil.

Industrialization (*see* DEVELOPMENT [INDUSTRIAL])

Industrial Waste

Industrial waste is material left over from processing raw materials into manufactured goods. Industrial wastes are an unavoidable result of human activities.

Industrial wastes may take the form of liquids, solids, or gases. Some, but not all, industrial wastes are toxic (poisonous). Other industrial wastes pollute the environment with greenhouse gases, heat, excess nutrients, or simply large quantities of harmless but unusable material. In order to preserve the quality of the earth's environment, industrial waste must be disposed of in a way that does the least amount of harm.

Infectious Wastes

Infectious wastes are materials that contain disease-causing bacteria or viruses. Most infectious wastes are produced in doctors' and dentists' offices, hospitals, and nursing homes. They must be handled very carefully, in order to prevent other people from catching disease (*see* MEDICAL WASTES). Spoiled food and farm animals that have died from disease are also considered infectious wastes.

Infrastructure

Infrastructure is the basic supporting framework around which a society is built. Roads, bridges, public buildings, rail lines, communications systems, pipelines, and power transmission lines are all part of our society's infrastructure.

A well-maintained infrastructure allows us to make efficient use of energy resources as we transport and use raw materials, products, and ourselves. Poorly maintained roads, bridges, and buildings are just one part of the breakdown of the quality of city life we call urban decay.

Inorganic

Inorganic describes material that does not come from living sources. Air, water, stone, and steel are examples of inorganic substances.

In chemistry, inorganic has a more specific meaning. It describes any chemical compound that does not contain carbon.

Insecticide

An insecticide is a poison that kills insects. Insecticides play an important part in modern farming. Many crops would be damaged or destroyed by insect pests without the use of insecticides. Insecticides are also used in homes to kill pests such as termites and cockroaches.

However, insecticides cause problems, too. They are often poisonous to wildlife (*see* DDT, KEPONE, for example). They can cause illness in farmworkers. Some insecticides may remain in the environment for long periods of time (*see* BIOACCUMULATION). And insects often adapt to an insecticide, forcing farmers to use heavier doses or new, more powerful poisons.

Instinct

Instincts are actions that animals perform automatically. Much of animal behavior is instinctive. For example, the nest-building and mating rituals of birds are instincts. So are the schooling behavior of fish and the migrations of caribou herds. Instincts help animals survive in their environment.

Instincts are not learned. They are inherited— passed on from parent to offspring. So when the

107

environment changes rapidly, instincts remain the same. Animals continue to use instinctive behaviors even when they are no longer useful. For example, some species of fish, like salmon and herring, instinctively return to their home rivers to spawn. If these rivers are blocked by dams or polluted, the fish still try to return rather than search for another place to lay their eggs. In such cases, instincts may play a part in a species becoming endangered or extinct.

Internal-Combustion Engine

The internal-combustion engine was developed in the late 1800s. It produces power by mixing gasoline or other fuel with air and then burning it inside metal cylinders. Each explosion of fuel provides force that turns the wheels of a car, spins the blades of a lawn mower, or does hundreds of other useful tasks.

These machines are an everyday part of modern life. But our dependence on internal-combustion engines creates huge environmental problems. The engines are quickly using up our supply of petroleum. And they produce great amounts of pollution. Because the fuel in internal-combustion engines is burned inside a closed space, it does not burn completely. Pollutants such as carbon monoxide and hydrocarbons come out in the engine's exhaust. The exhaust also contains lots of carbon dioxide, the main cause, scientists believe, of global warming.

In recent years, designers have made great improvements in internal-combustion engines, especially car engines. They create more power with less fuel and less pollution. Nevertheless, internal-combustion engines are still the biggest source of air pollution in the modern world.

Introduced Species (*see* EXOTIC SPECIES)

Inversion Layer (*see* TEMPERATURE INVERSION)

Ionizing Radiation

An atom that loses one or more electrons is called an ion. Ionizing radiation is any radiation strong enough to knock electrons away from an atom. X rays and gamma rays, alpha and beta particles, and neutrons are all considered ionizing radiation.

Ionizing radiation is produced in nuclear reactions such as those in nuclear power plants and nuclear explosions. It is part of radioactive fallout, and it is given off by all forms of radioactive waste. It is also given off by naturally radioactive elements such as uranium and radon.

Ionizing radiation is used in medical treatment, research, and industrial processes. It can also harm living things by ionizing atoms in the body. This changes the chemical makeup of the cells, causing radiation sickness and cancer.

Irrigation

Irrigate means to moisten with water. Irrigation allows people to grow crops in regions that don't get enough rainfall to support farming. Water for irrigation may come from rivers, lakes, or aquifers.

Farmers in many regions of the world irrigate their crops. Irrigation is widely used in the western United States to grow fruits, vegetables, grains, and cotton on land that would otherwise be desert.

Irrigation does cause problems, however. It drains water from its natural source. Groundwater levels in the western United States have been dropping because so much well water is used for irrigation. The great Colorado River that roars through the Grand Canyon is just a trickle by the time it reaches the Gulf of Mexico because so much of it is taken to irrigate crops. Irrigation may also require people to dam a natural river to form a lake, flooding a wilderness area in the process. Many years of irrigation can also leave a buildup of salts on the farmland, making the land less fertile (*see* SALINATION).

The Aral Sea, in the former Soviet Union, may be the worst example of the harmful effects of irrigation. It was once the world's fourth largest lake. But rivers flowing into the Aral Sea were used to irrigate surrounding land. By 1991, the Aral Sea had shrunk to one fourth its original size. Its fishing industry

Irrigation pipes like these allow farmers to grow crops in areas that lack sufficient rainfall, but irrigation can also cause numerous environmental problems.

was destroyed. Much of the land around it is so polluted with salts and pesticides that the area is now barren and useless.

Island

An island is a small area of land surrounded by water. Because islands are separated from other land, they are especially interesting to biologists. The biological community on every isolated island is unique. Species that can be found nowhere else on earth evolve on islands.

Charles Darwin developed his theory of evolution after seeing the different species of finches, tortoises, and iguanas that live on each of the separate Galápagos Islands. He realized that the different species had evolved from common ancestors. Each had adapted to the special conditions on its own island home.

Island creatures are protected by their isolation. But they have nowhere to escape from predators or from competing species. So they are easily endangered when exotic species are introduced. For example, flightless birds like the moa and the dodo evolved on islands in the south Pacific and Indian oceans, where there were no mammalian predators. After rats, pigs, and dogs were introduced by sailors, the moa and dodo birds soon became extinct. Many other island species face similar dangers today (*see* EXOTIC SPECIES, NATIVE SPECIES, NATURALIZED SPECIES).

Ivory

Ivory is the tusks of elephants, walruses, and several other mammals including whales. It has a creamy white color and a warm luster. Ivory has long been prized as a material for making piano keys, jewelry, and other decorative objects.

Unfortunately, ivory became so valuable that people have hunted ivory-bearing animals—especially African elephants—until they have become endangered. In 1989, the international trade in ivory was completely banned. Nevertheless, poachers continue to hunt elephants, and some traders continue to buy and sell their valuable tusks illegally.

James River (*see* KEPONE)

K-L

Kepone

Kepone is a long-lasting insecticide that was used to kill fire ants and other insect pests. It was made for the Allied Chemical Company by a small company called Life Science Products in Hopewell, Virginia. In 1975, many of Life Science's employees began getting ill. Unsafe working conditions exposed them to high levels of kepone. The entire work site was contaminated with the poison. The workers suffered from liver damage, nervous ailments, and sterility. Kepone carried home on workers' clothing had even made family members sick.

Kepone had also been discharged into Hopewell's sewage treatment plant. The kepone killed the sewage-digesting bacteria. So both untreated sewage and the kepone itself were dumped into the James River. The poison polluted the water and accumulated in the fish and wildlife along the river. Altogether, about 100 tons of kepone had been released into the air, water, and soil around Hopewell.

One hundred miles of the James River was closed to fishing and oyster gathering. Contaminated fish were also found in parts of the Chesapeake Bay. It was 13 years before fishing was again permitted in the river. Because kepone breaks down very slowly, thousands of pounds of the poison remain buried in the river sediments.

Allied Chemical paid a $5 million fine for illegal dumping. It paid another $6 million to establish a fund used to clean up the environment. But taxpayers still had to pay millions more to help with the cleanup. And the fishermen of eastern Virginia suffered years of economic loss.

Landfill

A landfill is a disposal site for solid waste such as household garbage or trash. Hazardous materials, such as industrial wastes or even low-level radioactive wastes, are buried in special landfills.

Trash is buried in a landfill and then covered with soil. Over the years, some of the trash buried in a landfill decomposes. But much of the material remains buried for hundreds of years without breaking down. When full, some landfills have been converted into parks and golf courses.

In the past, little concern was given to what happened after trash was dumped. However, modern landfills are often lined with clay or plastic and capped with waterproof covers. This helps to keep waste liquids from leaking into streams or groundwater. Landfills may also have vents to release gases that are produced as the trash decomposes.

In the United States, each of us produces about 1,500 pounds of household trash per year. As our growing population produces more trash, new landfill space has become much harder to find. Few people want landfills located in their communities. Recycling paper, metals, plastics, glass, and cardboard reduces the need for new landfill space (*see* SOLID WASTE).

Leach/Leachate

Leaching is the process by which rainwater and groundwater dissolve minerals and wastes and carry them away from their original site. The contaminated water is known as leachate.

Once wastes have leached into the surrounding groundwater, they are almost impossible to remove. The leachate flows away from the site, contaminating wells and streams.

Leaching is especially serious at toxic waste

sites. It is also a common problem in mining. Rain washes chemicals from the piles of tailings—waste ore and rock—that mining produces. This leachate, called acid mine drainage, pollutes streams and rivers in mining regions.

Lead (*see* HEAVY METALS)

Life Cycle

A life cycle is the process of birth, growth, reproduction, and death that every species goes through. The life cycles of different creatures show amazing variations.

For example, a fruit fly begins life as an egg that's been laid in a piece of ripening fruit. The egg hatches into a larva, called a maggot, that eats the fruit for several days. The maggot then forms a pupa and stays dormant for another few days while it changes into an adult fly. The adult fly mates, lays eggs, and then dies as the cycle begins over again. The entire life cycle of the fruit fly takes just a couple of weeks.

The life cycle of a mammal is very different. An elephant, for example, is born already in the form it will keep for its entire life. In its early years, it depends on its mother for nourishment and protection. It reaches maturity only after about 10 to 14 years. An elephant may have a number of offspring and live as long as 65 years.

Plants also have a wide variety of life cycles. Some plants reproduce with spores, others produce seeds, and still others send out runners or underground stems. Some plants, such as oak or hickory, take many years before they begin producing seeds. Other plants live for just a single season. They grow quickly, produce a crop of seeds, and then die.

Life Span

A life span is the average length of time that individuals of any species live. Life spans of creatures in the natural world vary widely, from just a few days to thousands of years. Adult mayflies emerge from the water of a stream, mate, lay their eggs, and die in a single day. On the other hand, there is a bristlecone pine tree in California that is believed to be 4,000 years old. In the past two centuries, the average human life span has been extended, thanks to advances in medicine and nutrition.

Litter

Litter is trash that people have thrown away carelessly, rather than disposing of properly. Litter is ugly and it can harm wildlife. For example, sea turtles mistake plastic bags for the jellyfish they like to eat. When they swallow the bags, their digestive systems become blocked and they die. Seabirds die when their necks are trapped in the plastic rings used to package six-packs of soda and beer.

Litter is also the term for the scattering of leaves and twigs that covers the forest floor. Leaf litter acts as a mulch. It eventually decays to form humus and enrich the soil.

Litter is also the word used to describe a group of animals born at one time to the same mother.

Littoral Zone

The littoral zone is the region at the very edge of the ocean: the seashore. The littoral zone extends from the rocks or beach exposed at only low tide to the farthest reach of sea spray.

The littoral zone is a demanding habitat. Plants and animals that live there are exposed to alternating

116

wet and dry periods and crashing waves. Neverthe-less, life thrives in the littoral zone. Tide pools and salt marshes teem with crabs, shrimp, mussels, bar-nacles, algae, and other plant and animal life. Even sandy beaches support an assortment of burrowing creatures that survive on the nutrients that the sea brings to them.

Love Canal

Love Canal is a section of Niagara Falls, New York. In the late 1970s, it became a symbol for the nation-wide problem of toxic waste disposal.

In the 1940s and 1950s, the Hooker Chemical Company used Love Canal as a dump for toxic wastes, including PCBs, dioxin, and pesticides. Later, houses were built on the filled-in land.

People who bought the homes didn't realize that they were built on a toxic dump. In 1978, resi-dents found poisonous wastes leaking into their basements. Tests showed that the residents had chromosome damage and other medical problems caused by exposure to the toxic waste.

People in the Love Canal neighborhood were forced to move. After a long legal battle, Hooker Chemical and the city of Niagara Falls had to pay the residents $20 million in damages.

M

Malthus, Thomas

Thomas Malthus (1766–1834) was a British economist. He developed the idea that human populations grow faster than their food supplies. According to this theory, people will always have to struggle for food. Improvement of the human condition is possible only if strict controls are put on population growth. This idea can also apply to other species.

Malthus wrote his ideas in a book called *An Essay on the Principle of Population as it Affects the Future Improvement of Society*, published in 1798. It is one of the most influential books in economics and in ecology.

Populations and food supplies don't grow at the exact rates that Malthus calculated. But the earth's human population has continued to grow faster than its ability to feed itself, as Malthus predicted.

Mariculture

Mariculture is the farming of marine (saltwater) species. Many marine creatures are very valuable as human food. Clams, shrimp, oysters, salmon, abalone, and edible seaweeds are all now grown with saltwater farming methods. Scientists are also trying to grow other valuable species like lobster and tuna.

Demand for these foods is very high—more than the world's oceans can sustain. Raising seafood through mariculture is a promising way to increase the world's food supply without overfishing wild populations of fish and shellfish (see AQUACULTURE).

Marine Environment

About 70 percent of the earth's surface is covered with water. The oceans are the planet's largest environment. Scientists believe that life on earth began in the oceans.

The oceans absorb most of the sunlight that strikes the earth's surface. Ocean water evaporated into the atmosphere provides most of the planet's rainfall. Ocean currents like the Gulf Stream carry solar energy from tropical regions to cooler parts of the globe. Plantlike phytoplankton produce much of the world's food and oxygen.

Scientists who study the marine (saltwater) environment often divide it into zones. These zones can be thought of as different biomes. The creatures that live in the littoral (beach) zone or in coastal waters are very different from those that live miles beneath the ocean's surface in the abyssal zone (*see* ZONATION).

Marine Mammals

Mammals are warm-blooded animals with backbones. They have hair, bear their young alive rather than laying eggs, and feed their young with the milk they produce from special glands. Marine mammals are mammals that live in saltwater environments. They include whales, dolphins, seals, sea lions, walruses, sea otters, and manatees.

Some marine mammals have been hunted almost to extinction for their meat, oil, and fur. Others, like manatees and some species of dolphin, have lost most of their habitat to human development.

In recent years, conservationists have made many efforts to protect marine mammals. For example, tuna fishermen often use dolphins to guide them to schools of tuna. As a result, dolphins were often trapped in the nets with the tuna and killed by the thousands. In the 1980s, consumers protested this practice by boycotting canned tuna. By 1990, the tuna packing companies had begun using new fishing methods that let the dolphins escape.

Strictly enforced boating speed limits now protect manatees in their remaining Florida habitats. To save baby fur seals, members of Greenpeace, an environmental organization, have sprayed them with dye to make them useless to hunters. Thanks to these and other actions, U.S. citizens have become more aware of the need to protect the earth's remaining marine mammals (*see* WHALES).

Marsh

A marsh is a wetland with low-growing plants like grasses or arums. Marshes are the most productive of all ecosystems. The shallow water of a marsh warms quickly. The roots of the marsh plants stabilize and build the soil, trapping new particles of mud and sand. The plants grow thickly, giving food and shelter to many small animals. The waters are full of algae and microscopic animal life. These small creatures

The waters of a marsh teem with animal and plant life. The wetland also provides habitat for migrating waterfowl.

become food for larger predators. Marshes also provide habitat for migrating birds such as ducks and geese. As marsh plants die and decay, they enrich the water with nutrients for more plant growth.

There are both freshwater and saltwater marshes, each type with its own distinctive plants and animals (see SALT MARSH).

Maximum Sustainable Yield

Maximum sustainable yield is the largest amount of a biological resource that can be harvested each season without reducing the amount harvested in following seasons. If we catch too many salmon or shrimp, for example, there won't be enough left to reproduce and replenish the supply for future years.

The European settlers of North America went far beyond the maximum sustainable yield when they hunted. As a result, the great herds of bison that roamed the prairie are gone. The passenger pigeon was hunted to extinction. More recently, yields of salmon, lobster, striped bass, and other species have dropped sharply because of overharvesting.

There is also a limited amount of forest land available, and it takes time for trees to grow. It's possible to cut so much timber that new trees won't be able to regrow enough wood to meet our needs. In some parts of the world—especially in Africa and Asia—humans have gone far beyond the maximum sustainable yield of the woodlands. Trees were cut down much faster than they could regrow. Now firewood is difficult to find, and some deforested areas have even turned into desert.

To preserve plant and animal resources, we must know what the maximum sustainable yield of each species is. Governments can then limit the catches of game, fish, and shellfish, or the harvesting of timber. Sometimes the season for a particular species

121

may be just a few days. Some species cannot be hunted at all until their populations increase. Unfortunately, it's hard to know just what the maximum sustainable yield of a species actually is. We may still be harvesting tuna, salmon, shrimp, or other species at rates that will prevent them from renewing their numbers.

Meat

Meat is the flesh of animals that we eat as food. It is a rich source of protein and other nutrients. However, raising animals for meat uses more resources than growing plant foods, such as wheat, rice, or soybeans. Raising animals for meat uses more than two thirds of all the agricultural land in the United States. Meat production uses at least ten times more fuel than growing grain crops, and at least ten times as much water.

Much of the tropical rain forest destroyed in recent years was cut down to create pasture for cattle. The grain now used to feed most animals would support many more people if it were fed to people directly.

Some animals are more efficient at changing grain into meat than others. For example, it takes about 2.5 pounds of feed to grow a pound of chicken. A pound of pork takes about 3.5 pounds of feed. Cattle are the least efficient meat producers: It takes 10 pounds of feed to produce just one pound of beef.

Because meat production uses so many resources, people in poorer nations eat much less meat than those in the industrialized world. Many environmentalists think we all should eat less meat—especially beef—and more grain products. That change would make better use of our planet's resources, protect some threatened rain forests, and make more food available for others.

Medical Wastes

Medical wastes are materials that may contain disease-causing bacteria or viruses. They are produced in doctors' and dentists' offices, hospitals, and nursing homes. Medical wastes include human blood, blood products, sharp medical tools such as syringes, and soiled articles such as sheets or bandages used by people who have infectious diseases.

Medical wastes must be disposed of properly to prevent other people from getting sick. The public has become much more concerned about medical wastes since the beginning of the AIDS epidemic. In 1988, used syringes washed up on beaches on the East Coast of the United States. Medical wastes were found in other public areas as well. State and federal agencies quickly strengthened the rules that cover disposal of such wastes.

Medical wastes get special handling. They are separated and placed in special containers. They must be disposed of so that there is no risk of infecting other people. Medical wastes are incinerated (burned) or disinfected with heat or chemicals before they are buried in landfills.

Mercury (*see* HEAVY METALS)

Methane

Methane is a gaseous fuel made up of carbon and hydrogen atoms. It is one of the gases that makes up natural gas. Methane is also produced in the intestines of animals as they digest food, and in decomposing organic matter.

Methane is also a greenhouse gas; in the atmosphere it traps heat and contributes to global warming.

123

Microwave Radiation

Microwaves are a kind of electromagnetic radiation. They have less energy than other forms of radiation such as visible light, ultraviolet radiation, and X rays.

Microwaves are used to send radio and television signals and in radar. In microwave ovens, they heat food by exciting (heating) its water molecules.

Microwaves are also produced by electrical equipment and appliances. Just as microwaves can cook food, they can damage human cells. Microwaves given off by electrical transmission lines or appliances such as televisions and electric blankets may cause medical problems, from nerve damage to cancers. Microwave ovens are shielded to prevent harmful radiation from escaping. Medical researchers are still trying to find out just how much harm the microwaves in our modern electrified environment are doing.

Migration

Migration is a two-way movement of animals that follows a regular pattern. Migration helps animals find food, shelter, warmth, or breeding grounds. In North America, the northward migrations of Canada geese are a sign of spring, and their southward return tells of the coming of winter.

Many birds migrate north and south each year to find feeding and nesting grounds. Locusts migrate to find food. North American monarch butterflies migrate south each fall. Salmon, shad, and herring migrate up freshwater rivers and streams to spawn. Caribou migrate from summer to winter grazing land. Whales migrate between summer and winter feeding grounds across thousands of miles of ocean.

Although we usually think of migrations as seasonal, some animals migrate back and forth daily. For example, crustaceans like shrimp and krill migrate vertically every day. They rise to feed in the productive surface waters each night, and then return to safer deep waters during the day.

Mimicry

Mimicry is a special form of protective coloration or camouflage. With mimicry, a species is protected by looking like another species that is dangerous or unpleasant to predators.

For example, there are flies that mimic the bright, striped markings of bumblebees. Bee flies have no sting, but their appearance discourages predators from attacking them. The nonpoisonous scarlet king snake has red, yellow, and black coloring that looks much like the poisonous coral snake.

The viceroy butterfly also protects itself through mimicry. The viceroy is perfectly edible to birds. But it has evolved to look like a monarch butterfly, which has a taste that birds don't like. Birds avoid eating the monarch, so the viceroy is protected, too.

Minamata, Japan (see HEAVY METALS)

Mining

Mining is the process of removing minerals and ores from the earth. Coal, metals and metal-bearing ores, gems, limestone, salt, and many other useful materials are taken from the earth through mining. We need these nonrenewable resources to supply industry and keep up our standard of living.

More than three million acres of U.S. land have been disturbed by mining activities. Most minerals are removed with surface mining methods like open-pit mines or quarries, rather than by underground mining.

Mining creates many environmental problems. It produces large piles of waste rock and used ore. Eight tons of waste rock are produced for each ton of coal mined, for example. In the United States, about 7.5 tons of mine wastes are produced per person each year. Mining is also one of the most dangerous occupations.

Mines also disturb water supplies. They increase the amount of erosion from the land. Rainwater and groundwater may dissolve sulfur compounds in the piles of mine wastes. This creates streams of acid mine drainage that poison nearby rivers. Mine drainage may also contain other poisons, such as arsenic or lead.

Monocropping/Monoculture

Monocropping or monoculture is the practice of planting large areas of land with a single crop. It is a destructive kind of farming.

Every type of crop uses certain nutrients in the soil. If the same crop is planted year after year, the soil is robbed of that nutrient and becomes less fertile. The practices of planting different crops and leaving farmland fallow (unplanted) during some years give the soil a chance to recover and rebuild its supply of nutrients.

Monoculture has another danger. If a disease or insect pest attacks the crop, it can quickly spread across a wide area and do great damage. That is less likely to happen if farmers plant smaller plots with a variety of different crops. If they've planted a variety of crops, losing one to bad weather or insect pests is less of a disaster.

Mutation/Mutagen

A mutation is a change in the genetic code of a cell. A

126

mutagen is any chemical that causes such hereditary changes.

When a mutation takes place in a reproductive cell, that change may be passed on to an organism's offspring. Occasionally a mutation may be useful— such as a better color for camouflage—and help the offspring survive. But most mutations are harmful. They cause the organism to develop some sort of birth defect.

Mutagens in our environment include radiation such as X rays, some viruses, certain drugs, cigarette smoke, mercury and lead compounds, and other industrial chemicals. There are probably many other mutagens not yet identified by researchers.

N

National Environmental Policy Act

The National Environmental Policy Act was passed by the U.S. Congress in 1969. It requires environmental impact statements for all major government projects, such as roads, bridges, canals, and dams. It also established the President's Council on Environmental Quality.

Native Species

Native species are the first species to live in a particular region of the world. Each native species has adapted to its habitat and developed defenses to protect itself from the predators and other dangers in its environment. The process of evolution has taken place over many thousands, or even millions, of years.

Native species of North America include the bison, rattlesnake, wild turkey, bald eagle, Pacific salmon, hickory tree, and chestnut tree, for example.

Native species can be threatened when other, exotic species are introduced into their habitat from elsewhere. The natives may not have evolved defenses against introduced predators or new diseases. For example, the native chestnut trees of North America have been almost completely destroyed by the chestnut blight, a fungus introduced from Europe (*see* EXOTIC SPECIES, NATURALIZED SPECIES).

Natural

Natural means coming from nature. The word often describes something left in its undisturbed state. For example, a stand of old growth forest could be called natural.

Natural also describes processes that take place

without human interference. The ecological succession as a meadow gradually becomes a woodland is a natural process. So is the act of predator eating prey as part of a complex food web.

Finally, the word *natural* is often used to describe a wide variety of products, from cereals to soaps. Many people believe that natural products are more pure and healthy for them than artificial, synthetic products. But in fact, most products advertised as being natural have been processed in some way. In advertising claims, the word *natural* generally has little meaning.

Natural Gas

Natural gas is a fossil fuel. It is the gaseous remains of sea creatures that lived many millions of years ago. These creatures were buried beneath layers of sedimentary rock. The pressure and heat eventually turned them to gas and oil. Deposits of petroleum and natural gas are often found together. Natural gas itself is composed mainly of methane, along with other hydrocarbon gases like ethane, butane, and pentane. Russia and the United States are the world's top two producers of natural gas.

Natural gas provides heat for homes and industry. It is also a raw material for making fertilizers, detergents, drugs, synthetic fibers such as nylon and polyester, and many other products. Natural gas burns more cleanly than gasoline or diesel oil. Cars and trucks with engines that burn natural gas produce less pollution.

Natural gas is a nonrenewable resource. At the current rate of use, the world will run out of natural gas by the middle of the 21st century.

Naturalized Species

A naturalized species is a type of organism that now

lives in a particular ecosystem, but evolved somewhere else. Naturalized species begin as exotic immigrants to a new ecosystem. Most naturalized species were introduced into an environment by people, either accidentally or on purpose. Naturalized species compete with the native species already living in an ecosystem.

For example, aggressive African honeybees were brought to Brazil in 1957 as an experiment to increase honey production. These bees (sometimes known as "killer" bees) escaped and became naturalized. Migrating at a rate of about 50 miles each year, they've spread north through South and Central America and have reached as far as south Texas.

Other naturalized species in North America include Japanese beetles, kudzu, honeysuckle, sparrows, starlings, rats, and the gypsy moth (*see* EXOTIC SPECIES, NATIVE SPECIES).

Natural Pest Control (see BIOLOGICAL PEST CONTROL)

Natural Selection

Natural selection is the process by which evolution takes place. A certain trait—color, size, shape, even a behavior—may help an individual plant or animal live more successfully. An organism that has this trait has an advantage. It is more likely to survive long enough to reproduce. That means it will also pass the trait on to its offspring.

Meanwhile, individuals that don't have the trait are less likely to survive and reproduce. They may be eaten by predators, for example. Over many generations, individuals with the trait become more common, while those without it die off. Through a *natural* process of survival, individuals that are better adapted are *selected* to reproduce and pass on their genes.

Suppose an animal is a little better camouflaged than others of its species. As a result, it has a better chance to survive and have babies. Those with poorer camouflage are more likely to be eaten before they reproduce. The babies that inherit the better camouflage trait are also more likely to survive and bear young. Over many generations, more and more individuals with the better trait survive. Eventually, the entire species evolves to become better camouflaged.

The process of natural selection is happening all the time, as animals and plants succeed or fail to reproduce. However, it works slowly, over many generations, so we rarely see it in action (*see* EVOLUTION).

Niche

A niche is the specialized place and role in an ecosystem occupied by one particular kind of organism.

For example, the niche of the blue mussel is the rocks below the high tide line to which it clings and filters microscopic food particles from the cool North Atlantic waters. The niche of the termite is the dead wood in which it lives, and which it also eats. Each individual species has its own special niche.

The niche of an organism includes both the specialized habitat in which it lives and the specialized way that it makes use of the resources in that habitat.

NIMBY

NIMBY stands for "Not In My Back Yard." Everyone wants to get rid of wastes, but nobody wants them dumped nearby. All of us want plenty of electricity, but we don't want a power plant built in our neighborhood. We want better roads, but we don't want the street in front of our house widened. NIMBY is a quick way to summarize that common attitude.

People usually support changes that improve the quality of their lives, unless the changes damage the environment in their own neighborhood, community, or state. Then they'll fight to prevent the changes. Whenever new projects are proposed, planners must expect to face local residents who oppose them.

Nitrogen Cycle

Nitrogen is a chemical element. The earth's atmosphere is 78 percent nitrogen. Nitrogen is one of the elements needed to build proteins in both plants and animals. The nitrogen cycle traces the path that nitrogen takes through the environment.

Plants and animals can't use the nitrogen in air directly. Plants must absorb nitrogen through their roots in the form of chemicals called nitrates and ammonia. Nitrogen from the atmosphere enters the upper layers of the soil as a gas or dissolved in rainwater. Nitrogen-fixing bacteria in the soil and blue-green algae change some of this nitrogen to nitrates, which plants can then use. Lightning bolts also produce nitrates that are washed into the soil when it rains.

Plants absorb nitrates from the soil and use them to build proteins. Animals get the nitrogen they need when they eat plants or other animals. When plants and animals die and decompose, the nitrogen in their bodies is released back into the soil to fertilize new plant growth. Animal manure is also rich in nitrogen.

The amount of nitrogen available in an environment is a major limit to its productivity. When there is more nitrogen in an environment, plants grow better. That also allows the environment to support more animal life.

Nitrogen Oxides

Nitrogen oxides are chemical compounds that pollute the air. They are produced when fuel is burned in automobiles, airplanes, furnaces, and factories.

Nitrogen oxides form a brownish haze in polluted city air. They irritate breathing passages. Combined with the water vapor in the air, they form nitric acid. The acid causes corrosion and contributes to acid rain. In the upper atmosphere, nitrogen oxides from airplane exhaust also damage the ozone layer.

Noise Pollution

Sound is simply vibrations transmitted through the air. The volume of sound is measured in units called decibels. Noise is unpleasant, unwanted sound.

Noise pollution is a widespread environmental hazard in modern society. Noise above the level of about 100 decibels (as loud as a nearby motorcycle or chainsaw) can gradually cause hearing loss. Noise above 130 decibels can cause severe and immediate damage to the delicate parts of the human ear. Loud noise can also make people irritable and less productive at work.

City dwellers in particular are bombarded with high noise levels from traffic, construction machinery, loud music, and many other sources. Workers who use noisy machinery must protect their ears or lose their ability to hear. People who listen to loud music, especially through headphones, face similar problems.

In many communities, local laws or regulations limit the amount of noise that people can be exposed to. New highways, airports, and construction projects often have to be designed to follow these rules.

Nonionizing Radiation

Nonionizing radiation includes visible light, ultraviolet radiation, infrared radiation, and microwaves. These forms of energy are not as powerful as ionizing radiation such as X rays and gamma rays. But some nonionizing radiation can still create environmental damage (*see* ULTRAVIOLET RADIATION, MICROWAVE RADIATION).

Nonrenewable Resources

Nonrenewable resources are resources that can't be replaced once they've been used. Coal, oil, and natural gas are nonrenewable resources. It takes millions of years for these fuels to form beneath the ground. Once they've been taken from the earth and burned, they cannot be replaced.

Mineral ores are also nonrenewable. Once iron ore has been mined, it cannot be replaced. Recycling products helps limit the amount of nonrenewable mineral resources that we use up.

Northern Coniferous Forest (*see* TAIGA)

No-Till Farming

No-till farming is a modern agricultural method. No-till means no plowing. Instead, a machine pulled by a tractor drills rows of shallow holes in an unplowed field. The machine drops a seed in each hole. Then it sprays the ground with a herbicide that keeps weeds from growing up and choking out the crop. Fertilizer may also be sprayed on the field at the same time.

134

In ordinary planting, the farmer first plows the field and then makes a second trip to break up the clods of soil with a disking machine. Finally, the tractor makes a third trip to plant the seeds. No-till farming does the entire job in just one trip. This saves time, money, and fuel.

Plowing can also create a soil condition called compaction or hardpan. When a field is plowed year after year, the soil just beneath the plowed ground becomes hard and tightly packed. Crops grow badly where there is a hardpan (*see* COMPACTION). No-till farming reduces that problem.

No till farming also reduces erosion. Bare top-soil is easily carried away by rain or wind. In no-till farming, the roots and stems from earlier crops help keep the soil in place and hold moisture in the soil.

No-till farming also has disadvantages. Plowing kills weeds by turning them under the soil. No-till farming uses powerful chemical weed killers instead. These poisons can also kill birds and other wildlife and may wash into nearby waterways and kill aquatic plants. These chemicals can also cause health problems for farmworkers if they are mishandled.

Not In My Back Yard (*see* NIMBY)

Nuclear Power

Nuclear power is electricity generated from the heat of uranium or plutonium atoms. These two elements are unstable. Their nuclei can split apart, releasing energy. When this happens in an uncontrolled chain reaction, the result is a nuclear explosion.

The same process that creates a nuclear explosion can be controlled in a nuclear power reactor. Uranium atoms split, releasing heat energy. This heat is used to change water to steam. The steam then spins a turbine, which drives an electrical generator.

The first commercial nuclear reactors were built in the 1950s. At that time, many people thought nuclear power was a cheap, safe energy source. Since plenty of uranium was available, it looked as though nuclear power could provide the world with electricity for hundreds of years. By 1992, there were 413 nuclear reactors producing commercial electrical power throughout the world.

However, nuclear power has turned out to be dangerous and expensive. Nuclear reactors can't explode like a bomb, but serious accidents can occur in which radioactive material is released into the environment. Because a nuclear accident can be so damaging, reactors must be carefully designed for safety. That makes them very expensive to build. Even with safeguards, there have already been several serious nuclear reactor accidents (*see* CHERNOBYL, THREE MILE ISLAND) and many minor ones.

Nuclear reactors also produce radioactive waste. This waste is difficult to handle and stays dangerous for thousands of years. The United States still has no permanent place to store it. After an operating life of only about 30 years, a reactor must be shut down and taken apart. This is also expensive and produces more radioactive waste.

For all these reasons, no U.S. power company has ordered a new reactor since 1973.

Nuclear Waste (*see* RADIOACTIVE WASTE)

Nuclear Weapons/Nuclear Weapons Production

The explosion of a nuclear weapon is a human tragedy and an environmental disaster. In 1945, the United States dropped the only two nuclear bombs ever used in warfare. They destroyed the Japanese cities of Hiroshima and Nagasaki and killed almost 200,000 people. A nuclear bomb destroys with intense heat, a powerful wave of explosive pressure, and radiation that remains in the environment for years.

The United States, Russia, China, Great Britain, France, India, Israel, and perhaps several other nations now have nuclear weapons. Other nations will soon be able to build them. Altogether, there are many thousands of nuclear weapons throughout the world. A war fought with even a few hundred of them could destroy much of human civilization. Much of the natural world would be destroyed as well.

In the past few years, the United States and Russia have reduced the number of nuclear weapons in their arsenals. But many remain, and nuclear weapons will be one of the earth's great dangers for years to come.

Even unexploded, nuclear weapons have caused huge environmental damage. Large amounts of toxic and radioactive waste have been produced merely by building bombs. The worst waste sites in the United States are located at nuclear bomb factories in Hanford, Washington; Rocky Flats, Colorado; Barnwell, South Carolina; and several other places around the country. These sites have old reactors, contaminated buildings, or huge tanks of poisonous, radioactive sludge. Even the soil and water are contaminated with toxic and radioactive chemicals. Cleaning up these old weapons factories will cost at least $300 billion. The waste will remain dangerous for many thousands of years. It will have to be buried deep beneath the ground, where it will never be disturbed or leak back into the environment.

Nuclear Winter

Some scientists predict that after a nuclear war, the earth's climate would cool drastically. Clouds of

137

smoke and dust would be thrown high into the air by the explosions and firestorms. These particles would remain in the upper atmosphere for months or years, blocking enough sunlight to lower the temperatures on earth. This period of lower temperatures is called nuclear winter. The theory of nuclear winter is based on the study of large fires and volcanic eruptions, which also throw dust and smoke into the air. In the past, volcanic eruptions have lowered the earth's average temperatures for an entire year or more.

In a nuclear winter, temperatures could drop so much that many plants would die. Without the food that plants provide, people and animals would starve. Chemicals in the dust clouds would also destroy much of the earth's ozone layer. This would allow the sun's ultraviolet radiation to reach the earth's surface, burning the eyes and skin of humans and animals, causing skin cancers, and also reducing plant growth.

Nutrient

A nutrient is any chemical element that an organism needs in order to live and grow. Plants and animals use nutrients to build new body tissue and to give them energy for their life processes.

The most important nutrients are oxygen, carbon, hydrogen, nitrogen, phosphorus, and potassium. Living things also need supplies of calcium, sulfur, and magnesium, as well as smaller amounts of other elements such as sodium, chlorine, zinc, iron, and copper.

Plants absorb the nutrients they need from the soil and the air. Animals get their nutrients from the food they eat.

O

Occupational Health and Safety

Environmental dangers are a part of many occupations. Some workers handle toxic materials as part of their jobs. Farmers use pesticides, for example. Painters are exposed to solvents; plumbers work with lead and other toxic metals. Many workplaces are filled with smoke or fumes. Workers may even bring toxic chemicals home on their clothing to contaminate their families.

Other workers are exposed to disease-causing substances. Many construction and shipyard workers have been exposed to asbestos, which causes lung cancer. Miners who breathe coal dust can develop black lung disease. Many medical and industrial workers are exposed to X rays or other radiation hazards.

Workers must have proper equipment and be trained to handle hazardous materials correctly. Otherwise, both the workers and the environment can be harmed.

Occupational Safety and Health Administration (OSHA)

The Occupational Safety and Health Administration (OSHA) is an agency of the U.S. Department of Labor. It began operating in 1971.

OSHA writes health and safety rules for the nation's workers. These rules cover fire prevention, protective clothing, proper ventilation, and many other areas of worker safety. OSHA also sets the maximum level of various poisons that workers are allowed to be exposed to.

139

OSHA is also responsible for enforcing its health and safety rules. In some states, OSHA inspectors check workplaces to make sure that the rules are being followed. In others, the state government takes that responsibility. Unfortunately, there are so many workplaces that health and safety inspectors can't check them very often. Unsafe practices can continue for months or years before they are discovered—perhaps not until they cause injury or death.

Ocean Thermal Energy Conversion (OTEC)

Ocean thermal energy conversion is an experimental method of generating electrical power. It uses the solar heat stored in ocean water. OTEC works much like a household heat pump.

The heat from warm surface water is used to vaporize a liquid chemical refrigerant. The pressure of the refrigerant gas turns a turbine to generate electricity. Then cold water from deeper in the ocean cools the refrigerant and condenses it back into a liquid. The refrigerant is then recycled back through the system.

To work effectively, OTEC needs at least 68°F temperature difference between the warm and cold water. So it is only practical in the tropics, where the surface waters stay warm year-round. OTEC also requires a convenient source of deep ocean waters that remain cool all year long. A small OTEC power station in Hawaii began operating in 1979. A year later, Japan started a similar project. OTEC is still experimental. However, it could become an important energy source because vast amounts of heat are stored in the world's ocean water.

Oil (*see* PETROLEUM)

Oil Sand/Oil Shale

Shale and sandstone are types of sedimentary rock. Oil shale and oil sand have petroleumlike hydrocarbons trapped within the rock itself. There are large deposits of oil shale in the western United States and in other parts of the world. A huge deposit of oil sand is located in western Canada.

Scientists and engineers are experimenting with practical ways to extract fuel from these rocks. The rock must contain at least 2.5 percent oil (about 10 gallons of oil per ton of rock) before it is worth processing for energy. Otherwise, mining and processing the shale use more energy than the rock produces. The oil from these rocks will be very expensive because of the work needed to mine and extract it. Getting oil from shale or sandstone also produces large amounts of waste.

As liquid petroleum reserves run out, these oily rocks will probably become more valuable. If better ways are found to extract the petroleum in oil shale and oil sand, these rocks could become important energy resources.

Oil Spill

Each year, millions of tons of petroleum are spilled into the world's oceans. On average, about one million tons of petroleum enter the seas through shipping accidents. Another four million to six million tons of petroleum and petroleum products leak into the oceans from pipelines, ship engines, leaky hulls, and natural vents in the earth's crust.

Oil spills kill wildlife. Petroleum products float on water. They are toxic to most living things. Oil spills lower the amount of dissolved oxygen in the water. They also reduce the amount of sunlight reaching marine plants. They coat the skin, feathers, and gills of sea animals. The feathers of oil-coated sea-

141

birds lose their insulating properties. Birds poison themselves when they clean the oil from their feathers with their beaks or die of exposure because the oily feathers can't keep them warm.

When oil coats the beaches, it smothers the creatures that live among the rocks and sand. Fish die from the oil itself or from lack of food. And of course, oil spills destroy the livelihoods of people who make their living from the sea.

As long as people ship oil around the world in tankers, there are sure to be oil spills.

The worst oil spill in North American history took place in 1989. The tanker *Exxon Valdez* struck a reef in Prince William Sound in southern Alaska. More than ten million gallons of crude oil spilled into the water. The cleanup cost more than $1 billion, but much of the region will remain polluted for years to come.

The world's worst oil spill came during the Persian Gulf War of 1991. The Iraqis dumped as much as 168 million gallons of oil into the Persian Gulf during that conflict.

Old Growth Forest

Old growth forest is climax woodland that has never been disturbed by logging or other human activities. Old growth forest has huge, mature trees and deep shade. Humus, leaf litter, and fallen limbs cover the forest floor. Old growth forest is sometimes called virgin forest.

There is almost no old growth forest in the eastern United States. Most eastern forest land was logged or used for farmland sometime in the past 300 years. There are still areas of old growth forest in the western United States and Alaska. Some are protected in national parks. Conservationists are trying to protect remaining old growth forests from logging

Organic

and preserve them as wilderness areas (*see* CLIMAX ECOSYSTEM).

Omnivore

An omnivore is an animal that eats both plant and animal foods. Human beings are omnivores. We eat both meats and fruits and vegetables. Other examples of omnivores include brown bears, box turtles, mice, and chimpanzees (*see* CARNIVORE, HERBIVORE).

OPEC (*see* ORGANIZATION OF PETROLEUM EXPORTING COUNTRIES)

Opportunism

Opportunism is a term that describes a species' ability to take advantage of, or adapt quickly to, changes in its environment. Raccoons are a good example of an opportunistic species. They can eat a wide variety of different foods, depending on what is available. And they've adapted well to changes in their environment. Raccoons evolved in the temperate forests of North America, but they now survive very successfully in the cities and suburbs of the United States.

Organic

The word *organic* has several different meanings. In everyday speech, organic usually describes something living, or material that comes from a living source. For example, cotton, wool, wood, and leather could all be described as organic.

In chemistry, organic has a special meaning. Any chemical that contains carbon is considered organic. Organic chemistry is the branch of chemistry that studies carbon compounds.

The word *organic* is also used to describe farming methods that don't use pesticides and artificial fertilizers (*see* ORGANIC FARMING/ORGANIC GARDENING).

Organic Farming/Organic Gardening

Organic farming and gardening is a collection of methods that some growers use to produce crops without chemical pesticides and fertilizers. Some people believe that the fruits, vegetables, and meats produced by organic farming are healthier to eat than those grown with chemicals.

Organic farmers fertilize their crops with manure and compost (decayed plant matter). They control insects by removing them by hand, by using nonpoisonous sprays such as soapy water or hot pepper solution, or by interplanting crops with other plants that insects don't like.

The crops of organic gardeners are usually not as pretty-looking as those from other gardens. The fruits and vegetables have some insect damage. But even so, organic gardeners believe that their crops are better because they contain no poisons or other chemicals.

Organism

An organism is any individual living thing.

Organization of Petroleum Exporting Countries (OPEC)

OPEC is a loosely organized group of countries that share a common resource—petroleum. The members of OPEC include Iran, Iraq, Saudi Arabia, Kuwait,

144

Libya, Nigeria, and Venezuela, and several other, smaller nations. Among them, OPEC nations produce about half of the world's petroleum.

OPEC was founded in 1960. Its purpose is to protect the profits of member countries. The organization tries to set oil prices and quotas for how much will be produced. OPEC has not been very effective in this effort in recent years. That's because individual member countries often act on their own in order to make as much income as they can.

OSHA (*see* OCCUPATIONAL SAFETY AND HEALTH ADMINISTRATION)

Overgrazing

Overgrazing is the practice of allowing too many goats, sheep, or cattle to feed in a pasture or woodland. Too many grazing animals eat the plants faster than the plants can grow new leaves. They eat more than the maximum sustainable yield of the land.

When land is overgrazed, many of the plants die. The few plants that are left afterward are those that the animals can't eat. Overgrazing causes erosion because there are fewer leaves to soften the impact of the rain and fewer roots to hold the soil. Because plants also hold moisture in the soil, overgrazing in regions of little rainfall can turn fertile land into desert.

Overpopulation

Overpopulation is a situation in which there are not enough resources in an ecosystem to support the number of individuals living in it. When a species is overpopulated, its ecosystem is out of balance. Individuals run out of food and shelter. Other species that provide food or compete for the scarce resources also suffer. Balance is restored when some of the population migrates to other habitats or dies.

No one is sure what the ideal human population of planet earth is or how many people the earth can support before it is overpopulated. We may have already passed the point of overpopulation. The earth's resources are quickly being used up, and a billion people are already underfed or starving.

Oxygen

Oxygen is a colorless, odorless gas that makes up about 21 percent of the earth's atmosphere. Oxygen is necessary for life on earth. Organisms use oxygen in respiration (breathing). Oxygen is taken into the body through lungs, gills, the skin, or cell walls. It is used to turn food into energy. The main waste products of this process are carbon dioxide and water.

The oxygen in the air is supplied by green plants. Plants release oxygen into the air as a product of photosynthesis—the process by which they make food using water, carbon dioxide, and sunlight (*see* DISSOLVED OXYGEN).

Ozone

Ozone is a special form of oxygen. Its chemical symbol is O_3. Ordinary oxygen molecules contain two oxygen atoms. Ozone molecules contain three.

Ozone is very chemically active. It is sometimes used as a bleach or a water purifier. Ozone is produced naturally in the atmosphere all the time. Both solar radiation and lightning cause ordinary oxygen in the air to form small amounts of ozone.

At ground level, ozone is a pollutant. It is produced in smog, when sunlight causes ordinary oxygen to react with pollutants in the air. Ozone causes headaches and irritation of the eyes and breathing passages. It also damages rubber and plastics.

However, ozone in the upper atmosphere is needed for life on earth (*see* OZONE LAYER).

Ozone Layer

The ozone layer is a region of the stratosphere that contains high concentrations of ozone gas. Ozone reaches its highest concentration about 19 miles above the earth.

Ozone absorbs the ultraviolet (UV) radiation in sunlight. The ozone layer keeps much of this damaging form of light from reaching the earth's surface.

UV radiation—also known as ultraviolet light—can be very harmful. UV radiation causes sunburn. It can damage or blind the eyes of people and animals and can cause skin cancer. Too much UV light also causes plants to grow poorly.

Some of the ozone in the upper atmosphere is being destroyed. Several years ago, scientists even discovered a "hole" in the ozone layer over the South Pole. In this region, the atmosphere's ozone was almost completely gone. The main cause of this problem is chlorofluorocarbon (CFC) pollution. Chlorofluorocarbons, which are used in refrigeration, destroy ozone molecules (*see* CFCs). Nitrogen oxides from the exhaust of jet engines also destroy ozone.

Life on earth would be very difficult without the protection of the ozone layer. So it is important for people to understand why it is disappearing and to take steps to stop that process.

147

P

Parasite

A parasite is an organism that takes its food from another organism that it lives on. The organism that provides the nourishment is called the host. A parasite is different from a predator because it doesn't ordinarily kill its host. However, it may take enough nutrients to weaken the host and make it unable to fight off diseases or predators.

Parasites are common throughout the living world. There are animal parasites, plant parasites, fungus parasites, and protist parasites. Tapeworms are parasites that live in the stomachs of animal or human hosts. They feed on the food that the host itself eats. Eggs from the tapeworm pass through the gut of the host and remain in the animal's droppings. When other animals eat food contaminated with the droppings, they become infected, too.

Mistletoe is another example of a parasite. A mistletoe seedling sinks its roots into a branch of a tree. There it grows, taking nutrients from the sap of its host. Athlete's foot, a fungus that lives on the human skin, is yet another example of a parasite.

Particulates

Particulates, also known as aerosols, are tiny bits of solid or liquid materials suspended in the air. Particulates are one of the components of air pollution. They come from the burning of fuels for heat and transportation and from industrial processes and farm activities. Fires and natural sources such as pollen and blowing dust also contribute particulates to the air.

Recent scientific studies suggest that particulates cause many thousands of deaths each year, especially among children and elderly people with breathing problems (*see* AIR POLLUTION).

Parts Per Thousand (PPT), Parts Per Million (PPM), Parts Per Billion (PPB)

These three terms give scientists a way to measure how much of a substance is contained in water, air, or some other material. For example, the concentration of salt in seawater is about 35 ppt. That means that every kilogram of seawater contains 35 grams of salt.

Imagine mixing a tablespoon of food coloring into a five-gallon bucket of water. The water would then contain about 1 part per thousand (1 ppt) of food coloring. Mixing a tablespoon of food coloring into a full-size swimming pool would give a concentration of about 1 part per million (1 ppm).

Scientists often use ppm or ppb to measure the level of pollution of water, soil, air, or food. This measure is also used in setting acceptable limits for contamination. (*See* PCBS for an example of how this method is used.)

Pathogen

A pathogen is a disease-causing organism. Any bacterium, virus, fungus, or other microorganism that causes a disease in humans, animals, or plants is considered a pathogen.

PBB (Polybrominated Biphenyl)

PBB is a toxic chemical used to prevent fires. In 1974, PBB was accidentally mixed with cattle feed in Michigan. As a result, a number of cattle died and thousands were contaminated with the chemical and had to be killed. No one is sure how much beef from contaminated cattle reached the marketplace.

PBB doesn't break down quickly in the environment. Because it is so stable, PBB pollution continued for years in some Michigan farms—in the soil, in the buildings, even in dust in the air. The Michigan Department of Agriculture had to test cattle for traces of the poison through the early 1980s.

PCBs (Polychlorinated Biphenyls)

PCBs are a group of oily, fire-resistant chemicals used in electrical transformers, in making plastics, and in several other important industrial processes. They pollute the environment in factory wastes, when transformers leak, when plastics are burned, and in other ways.

Experiments suggest that PCBs cause birth defects, cancer, and liver, nerve, and skin disorders. The FDA (Food and Drug Administration) currently allows food to contain no more than 2 ppm (parts per million) of PCBs. Production of PCBs was banned in the United States in 1979.

PCBs don't break down quickly in the environment. Instead, they accumulate in the bodies of animals and become concentrated at the top of the food chain. The Great Lakes are badly polluted with PCBs. Trout from Lake Michigan have PCB levels as high as 25 ppm.

Many waste disposal sites are badly contaminated with these chemicals. Devices such as electrical transformers containing PCBs are still in use. As they wear out and are disposed of, more PCBs will leak into the environment. And many tons of PCBs are still buried in the sediments of lakes and rivers. PCBs will continue to be an environmental problem for many years.

PCV System

A PCV system is an air pollution control device in

automobile engines. PCV stands for positive crank-case ventilation. Automobile makers began install-ing PCV systems in all new cars in 1963.

The crankcase of an engine is full of oil and exhaust gases. The PCV valve removes exhaust gases from the crankcase and passes them back through the engine. This burns the fuel more completely, cutting down on the amount of air pollution—especially hydrocarbons—that comes out of the car's tailpipe.

Pelagic Zone

The pelagic zone is the open ocean environment. Animals that swim in the open waters and are not ordinarily found either near the shore or the ocean bottom are pelagic organisms. For example, tuna, marlin, and krill spend their lives in the open ocean. They are considered pelagic species. Oceanographers subdivide the pelagic environment into zones by depth or nearness to land.

Pesticide

A pesticide is any poison that kills plant or animal pests. Pesticides are widely used in farming and home gardening. U.S. farmers use about 500 million pounds of pesticides each year.

Pesticides used to kill weeds are called herbi-cides. Pesticides that kill insects are called insecti-cides. Pesticides that kill rats and mice are called rodenticides.

Pesticides must be used carefully. They can have unwanted effects. They may kill other creatures in addition to the pests they were intended to control. Insecticides often kill helpful insects along with the insect pests. Most substances that kill pests are also poisonous to humans. The manufacture of pesticides also produces toxic industrial wastes.

151

Most foods we eat contain tiny amounts of the pesticides used in growing them. Organic farmers try to replace chemical pesticides with other methods of pest control that are less harmful to the environment (*see* ORGANIC FARMING/ORGANIC GARDENING).

Petrochemicals

Petrochemicals are products made from petroleum or natural gas. Many of these products are important to our modern economy. Petrochemical products include fertilizers, plastics, artificial rubber, medicines, paints, and fibers such as nylon and polyester. As the earth's nonrenewable supply of petroleum is used up, supplies of petrochemicals will also become scarce and expensive.

Petroleum

Petroleum, or crude oil, is a fossil fuel. It is the oily remains of sea creatures that lived several hundred million years ago. These creatures were buried under sea sediment. Time, heat, and pressure transformed them into petroleum.

Petroleum is often measured in barrels. One barrel is equal to 42 gallons. The United States uses over 17 million barrels (714 million gallons) of petroleum a day.

Human beings have come to depend on petroleum over the past 100 years. Petroleum products include gasoline, diesel fuel, heating oil, and lubricating oils. We use these fuels to heat our homes, generate electricity, and power our vehicles. Modern agriculture relies very heavily on petroleum products. Petroleum is also a raw material for thousands of products, including clothing, fertilizers, tires, and medicines (*see* PETROCHEMICALS).

Petroleum is a limited, nonrenewable resource.

At the rate petroleum is now being used, it's estimated that the world has only another 40 to 50 years of this resource left. Unless we find other sources of energy to take its place, life will change drastically once the reserves of petroleum are used up. We will have much less energy to transport ourselves, grow our food, and keep us warm.

Pets

Throughout the world, people keep animals as pets. This human activity has many, often harmful effects on the environment. Some pets, such as cats, are predators that hunt and kill wildlife (*see* CATS). Pets use food resources that might otherwise be used to feed people. Some pets can carry diseases; in cities, dog and cat droppings cause sanitation problems.

If exotic pets escape or are set free in a new habitat, they may cause problems for the creatures already living there. For example, in 1991, a shipment of 1,000 banana rasp snails was brought to the United States from Africa to be sold as pets. These snails are seven inches long. They are very destructive to garden crops. What's more, a single snail can reproduce asexually, without a mate. Federal investigators spent many months tracking down and destroying as many of the snails as they could find, but some were never located. If they escaped or were set free, they could become a severe agricultural problem.

Responsible pet owners must limit the environmental damage that their pets can do.

pH

pH is a measure of how acidic or basic a substance is. The abbreviation *pH* stands for "*percentage of Hydrogen ions.*" Hydrogen ions cause a substance to have acidic properties.

153

Chemists measure pH on a 14-point scale. Something with a pH of 7 is neutral—neither acidic nor basic. A pH of less than 7 is acidic; a pH greater than 7 means that a substance is basic.

Acidic substances include things like coffee (pH 5) and lemon juice (pH 3). Sulfuric acid, one of the strongest acids known, has a pH of 0. Ordinary rainwater is slightly acidic, with a pH of about 5.6. The pH of acid rain can be 4.0 or even lower. Basic, or alkaline, substances include baking soda (pH 9), soap (pH 10), and lye (pH 14).

Measuring pH is an important part of soil and water tests. Plants and animals are sensitive to pH. Some plants prefer mildly acidic soil, but most plants grow well only if the soil is slightly basic. If a pond or river is too acidic—because of acid rain, for example— most plants and animals can't live in it.

Phosphorus/Phosphates

Phosphorus is a chemical element. It is an essential nutrient for plants and animals. Phosphorus is used to build fats and oils, bones and teeth. It is also part of DNA molecules, which carry hereditary information. And it is used in cell metabolism—the process by which food is converted to energy.

Plants take up phosphorus through their roots in the form of phosphates (chemical compounds that include phosphorus and oxygen). Animals get phosphorus from the foods they eat.

Phosphorus enters the environment from mineral deposits. Phosphates are recycled through the environment as they pass through the food web (*see* PHOSPHORUS CYCLE).

Phosphates can also pollute the environment. Some detergents contain phosphates. When wastewater containing these detergents runs off into lakes or streams, the extra nutrients can cause a bloom of algae and plants. Such a bloom can choke a waterway. When the plants die and decay, they rob the water of oxygen.

In the 1970s some cities and states banned detergents that contain phosphates to prevent such pollution. Detergent manufacturers have lowered the amount of phosphates in many of their products and developed other detergents that contain no phosphates at all.

Phosphorus Cycle

The phosphorus cycle is the pathway that phosphorus takes as it passes through the environment and the food web. Phosphorus in mineral deposits and the soil is taken up by plants. Animals use the phosphorus in the food they eat to build bones, fat, and other tissues. Phosphorus is returned to the soil in animal droppings or when an animal dies and decays. The phosphorus is then available to be absorbed by plant roots once again.

Some dead plants and animals fall to the bottom of deep lakes or oceans, where they are buried under sediments. The phosphorus content of these organisms becomes a new mineral deposit and may be removed from the cycle for millions of years.

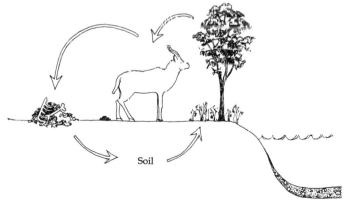

Soil

Phosphorus Buried
in Ocean Sediment

155

Photochemical Smog (*see* SMOG)

Photosynthesis

Photosynthesis is the process by which plants make food. It turns water and carbon dioxide into starches and sugars. Photosynthesis is a complicated chemical reaction with many steps. It starts when chlorophyll—the green pigment in plants—absorbs the energy from sunlight. Photosynthesis uses about 1 to 2 percent of the solar energy that reaches the earth's surface.

The final products of photosynthesis—sugars and starches—are chemical storehouses of solar energy. They provide food energy for plants, and for all animals as well. Through photosynthesis, plants also remove carbon dioxide—a greenhouse gas—from the air. Photosynthesis also produces the oxygen that animals need to breathe.

Phytoplankton

Phytoplankton refers to the small green plants and plantlike single-celled organisms that live in the upper layers of the world's oceans and lakes. Diatoms are the most common type of phytoplankton.

In nutrient-rich waters, phytoplankton turn the ocean a murky green color. Phytoplankton need sunlight, warmth, and plenty of nutrients to grow. The waters around tropical islands are a clear blue color because there aren't enough nutrients to support much phytoplankton growth.

Like other plants, phytoplankton make starches and sugars through photosynthesis. They also take up carbon dioxide and release oxygen as part of this process. Phytoplankton can only survive in the upper layers of the water, where plenty of sunlight is available.

Phytoplankton are an essential part of the world's ecosystem. More than 70 percent of the earth's surface is covered with water. Phytoplankton provide a major part of the oxygen in our atmosphere. And phytoplankton are the base of the oceanic food web. Either directly or indirectly, all animals living in the sea depend on phytoplankton for their food supply.

Plankton

Plankton refers to a wide variety of small organisms that float in the upper layers of salt or fresh water. Plankton include plants (phytoplankton), animals (zooplankton), and single-celled protists. Some planktonic creatures are the developing young of larger creatures such as crabs, shrimp, and oysters. Many other creatures live their entire lives floating about in the water as plankton.

Plankton are an essential part of life on earth. They are the base of the food chain for aquatic creatures. Phytoplankton also produce much of the earth's oxygen (*see* PHYTOPLANKTON, ZOOPLANKTON).

Plants

Many-celled organisms that make their own food through photosynthesis are classified as members of the plant kingdom. This kingdom includes mosses, algae, ferns, and seed-producing plants, including trees and shrubs.

Plants live in one place, without the ability to move. Although they may respond to stimuli such as light or touch, plants don't have a nervous system. They reproduce with seeds or spores, or spread asexually.

Almost all plants contain chlorophyll. Using solar energy, they change water and carbon dioxide into starches and sugars. Plants also give off oxygen in this process. This replaces the oxygen in the air that is used in respiration and decay.

Because they make their own food, plants are called the producers in any ecosystem. They are the first step in every food chain.

Plutonium

Plutonium is a heavy, radioactive metal. It is not found naturally on earth. It is produced from uranium in nuclear reactors. Plutonium is the explosive fuel in nuclear weapons. It takes only about 10 pounds of plutonium to make a nuclear bomb. Many thousands of pounds of plutonium have been made in the past 50 years, in nuclear weapons factories and as waste from nuclear power reactors.

Plutonium is very chemically active and burns when exposed to air. It has a radioactive half-life of 24,100 years. That means that after 24,100 years, half of a sample of plutonium will have changed into other elements through radioactive decay.

Plutonium is perhaps the deadliest substance known. A microscopic speck of plutonium can cause lung cancer. Because it is so dangerous and long-lasting, plutonium must be handled with extreme care. Safely disposing of wastes that contain plutonium is a problem that the U.S. government has yet to solve (*see* RADIOACTIVE WASTE).

Pollutant/Pollution

A pollutant is anything entering the environment that causes harm to the creatures living in it. Pollutants include synthetic chemicals and wastes poured into the air, water, or soil. Extra heat from power plants also causes pollution. So do the extra nutrients that run into rivers and lakes from fertilizers, detergents, or wastewater. Erosion can pollute a waterway with mud and silt. Radioactive wastes are another form of pollutant.

Pollution can also come from natural sources. For example, a red tide is a bloom of microscopic one-celled creatures called dinoflagellates. These organisms produce a poison that can kill fish and other marine creatures. A volcanic eruption can produce air and water pollution, as well as thermal (heat) pollution.

Pollution Control Device

A pollution control device is any machine that limits or removes pollutants from an engine, factory, or other pollution-creating process (*see* CATALYTIC CONVERTER, ELECTROSTATIC PRECIPITATOR, PCV SYSTEM, SCRUBBER, SMOKESTACK, VAPOR RECOVERY SYSTEM).

Polystyrene Foam

Polystyrene foam is usually known by the brand name Styrofoam. It is a light plastic filled with tiny air spaces. Polystyrene foam is used for insulation in homes, trucks, refrigerators, and coolers. It is also used as a packing material; some fast-food containers and disposable plates and cups are also made of polystyrene foam.

According to recent estimates, polystyrene foam takes up less than 1 percent of the space in U.S. landfills. At one time, some polystyrene foam was made using CFCs, gases that destroy the ozone layer. However, that is no longer true. Nevertheless, consumers are still concerned about this material. Because it is long-lasting and doesn't break down in the environment, foam litter is very noticeable.

In response to consumer complaints, some companies have switched from polystyrene foam to paper or cardboard packaging.

Population

A population is a group of the same species living in a particular area or region. Populations are measured with a count known as a census. A population study includes such information as birth and death rates, population spread, and population density (how many individuals live within a certain area).

In the natural world, populations tend to reach a point of balance. A region can support only a limited number of individuals. When the population of a species gets too large, it begins to run out of food. Overcrowding may also result in more disease. Part of the population then dies off. When a population of a species is small, more food becomes available. More individuals will survive and reproduce, and the population increases again.

Of course, the population of one species depends on the populations of many others—predators, prey, and other species competing for the same resources. Populations also change as seasons, climate, and other abiotic factors in the environment change. So the study of populations is a very complex subject.

In the past few thousand years, humans have been very successful in competing for habitat and food supplies. As a result, the populations of many other species have gotten much smaller or disappeared, and human populations have increased tremendously.

Population Control (*see* BIRTH CONTROL)

Population Explosion/Population Crash

A population explosion is a rapid increase in the size of a population of organisms. A crash is a rapid drop in the size of a population. Population explosions occur when there are abundant supplies of nutrients and other resources available. For example, when extra nutrients are added to a lake or river, a population explosion of algae can occur. When the resources run out, a population crash may follow as many individual creatures die.

The world has experienced a population explosion of human beings in the past 200 years. Because of advances in medicine, agriculture, and technology, the planet now supports more people than ever before. The world's human population is doubling every 41 years. In 1850, the world's population was about 1 billion. In 1990, it was about 5.5 billion. At this rate, there will be 10 billion people living on the earth by 2030.

No one is sure how large a human population the earth can support. A billion people in the world's poor nations are just barely surviving. The human population may already be headed for a crash as our planet's resources are used up.

Our population can't continue to grow forever. As more humans use the planet's resources, other species are becoming endangered or extinct. The human population explosion is one of the world's greatest environmental problems.

Potassium

Potassium is a chemical element. It is an essential plant nutrient and one of the three main ingredients in fertilizers. Plants take potassium from the soil through their roots. Animals also need potassium to carry on their normal body functions. Animals get their supplies of potassium through the foods they eat.

PPB, PPM, PPT (*see* PARTS PER THOUSAND)

Prairie (*see* GRASSLAND)

Precipitation

Precipitation is water from the air that condenses and falls to earth as rain, snow, sleet, or hail. The amount of precipitation in an ecosystem is one of the most important factors in determining how much and what kinds of life it can support.

Regions with heavy precipitation, such as tropical rain forests, are very productive. Heavy rainfall encourages abundant plant growth. The plants can feed large numbers of animals. Dry regions—deserts, chaparral, and grasslands—support many fewer plants and animals.

The timing of precipitation is also important. Some regions get precipitation regularly throughout the year. Others receive most of their precipitation during one short season. The living creatures in an ecosystem must adapt to the amount and timing of precipitation in order to survive.

Precycle

Precycling is a way to reduce the amount of solid waste that people throw away. Recycling means reusing waste products. Precycling means creating less waste in the first place.

Here are some things that people can do to precycle:

- Carry groceries home in reusable shopping bags.

- Choose products that have the least amount of packaging.

- Buy products in bulk amounts. (A five-pound box of macaroni uses less packaging than five one-pound boxes.)

• Buy products in packages that can be recycled or that are made of recycled materials.

• Choose products that are made from renewable resources, rather than from non-renewable resources.

The more precycling people do, the less waste they have to throw away and the easier it is to recycle what's left. The formal term for precycling is source reduction.

Predator

A predator is an animal that hunts and feeds on other animals. Wolves, cats, hawks, bass, sharks, and praying mantises are all examples of predators. The animals that a predator eats are known as its prey. Predators in an ecosystem are also known as secondary consumers (*see* CARNIVORE, CONSUMER).

Preservation (*see* CONSERVATION)

Prey (*see* PREDATOR)

Primary Consumer (*see* CONSUMER, HERBIVORE)

Prince William Sound (*see* OIL SPILL)

Producers

Producers are the organisms in an ecosystem that make their own food from the raw materials in their environment. Green plants and algae are the producers in any environment. They use air, water, sunlight, and minerals to produce food.

Plants produce food for their own growth. In addition, they are the base of every food chain, producing food for the animal consumers that depend on them for nourishment either directly or indirectly.

Propellant (*see* AEROSOL)

Protective Coloration (*see* CAMOUFLAGE, MIMICRY)

R

Radiation

Radiation is the energy source given off by substances. Every object in the universe gives off some form of radiation. Most often this takes the form of heat. Objects on earth warm up as they absorb solar radiation during the day. They lose energy and become cooler at night as they radiate the heat energy back into the space around them.

Visible light is also a form of radiation. So are radio waves, ultraviolet (UV) radiation, and the powerful X rays and gamma rays given off by radioactive materials.

Plants use the radiant energy of visible light to power the process of photosynthesis. UV radiation and the powerful radiation from nuclear reactions can be very harmful to living creatures. UV radiation from the sun causes sunburn and skin cancer. X rays and gamma rays can cause cancers and even changes in cell structure, called mutations (*see* IONIZING RADIATION, MICROWAVE RADIATION, ULTRAVIOLET RADIATION).

Radioactive Waste

The radioactive materials left over from nuclear power reactors, nuclear bomb production, and medical and industrial uses are called radioactive waste. Uranium mining also produces thousands of tons of radioactive waste each year.

Nuclear radiation damages body tissues, killing cells and causing burns and cancer. Exposure to large doses of radiation can be deadly. So radioactive waste—sometimes known as nuclear waste—must be handled and disposed of very carefully.

Radioactive waste is divided into several categories, depending on its source and the amount of

165

radiation it gives off. Some kinds of radioactive waste are much more dangerous than others.

The most dangerous radioactive wastes are spent (used) fuel from nuclear power reactors and high-level wastes from nuclear bomb factories. Reactors have already created more than 100,000 tons of this deadly waste, and more is being made every day. It stays dangerous for many thousands of years. Disposing of it safely is a huge problem. Highly radioactive waste must be buried where it will *never* be disturbed or leak into the environment. Right now, the United States has only temporary storage sites for its most dangerous radioactive waste. A permanent disposal site won't be ready until 2010 at the earliest.

Low-level radioactive waste from industry, hospitals, and scientific research is now buried in special landfills. The radiation from these wastes is still dangerous, but it is not as intense or as long-lasting. Special containers and methods must be used to make sure that this waste doesn't leak and contaminate the environment (*see* NUCLEAR POWER, NUCLEAR WEAPONS).

Radon

Radon is a colorless, odorless radioactive gas. It is produced naturally in the ground in rock or soil that contains small amounts of uranium. As the uranium breaks down through radioactive decay, it releases radon gas.

Radon is an environmental problem when it collects in buildings where people live or work. Breathing small amounts of radon can cause lung cancer. The soil in some areas releases radon gas that can leak into the basements of buildings and contaminate the inside air.

The air in homes and offices can be tested to see if it has dangerous levels of radon. If it does, the buildings can be ventilated or sealed to remove the problem.

Rainfall (*see* PRECIPITATION)

Rain Forest (*see* TEMPERATE RAIN FOREST, TROPICAL RAIN FOREST)

Rain Shadow

A rain shadow is an area of low rainfall on the downwind side of a mountain range. Air cools as it blows across tall mountains. The water in the air condenses to form rain or snow. As the winds then continue over the mountains, the air is much drier. The land beyond the mountain range gets very little rainfall.

In North America, the winds ordinarily blow from west to east. Along the West Coast, the wind carries moisture from the Pacific Ocean. It blows across the Coastal Range and the Sierra Nevada mountains. The air cools as it travels over these high mountains and drops its moisture as rain or snow. As

Wind

Ocean   Mountains   Desert

167

a result, the western sides of the mountains have a damp climate. But on the eastern side, the climate is extremely dry, with just a few inches of rainfall per year. Desert areas, therefore, are often formed in the rain shadow of the mountains.

Recycle

Recycle means to reprocess materials people have used and use them again. Recycling saves natural resources. It also saves the energy needed to process raw materials into products. And recycling lowers the need for landfill space, because less waste is thrown away.

Many common products can be recycled: paper, cardboard, glass, metals (including aluminum, steel, and copper), clothing, yard wastes, and some plastics. Machines and appliances can be repaired and recycled instead of being thrown away. Recycling paper and cardboard means that the paper industry cuts down fewer trees. Recycling aluminum containers means that industry will use much less energy to process new ore into metallic aluminum.

By 1990, almost two thirds of all aluminum cans were being recycled. Recycling aluminum saves up to 95 percent of the energy needed to produce new aluminum. The energy savings from other recycled materials is not as great. Recycled glass saves only about 30 percent of the energy needed to make new glass, for example.

Many cities and towns now have recycling programs. A good recycling program needs to be convenient and rewarding. Otherwise, many people won't bother to participate. Curbside pickup makes it easy for people to recycle. Paying for recycled materials also encourages them to get the recycling habit. Recycling companies pay well for aluminum and other metals, for example. Deposits on bottles, cans, and other containers also encourage recycling. If landfills charge by weight or by the container for trash disposal, more people will recycle to save money.

Renewable Resource

A renewable resource is any raw material that can be replaced or regrown after it has been used. Renewable resources are not permanently destroyed when they are used, as coal or oil are.

Trees are a renewable resource. After they have been harvested for human use, more trees can be grown to replace those that have been cut. Water supplies are also renewable resources, as are solar and wind energy, farm products, and fish and seafood.

Renewable resources still must be cared for. Rivers and aquifers can become polluted. Forestland can erode after a crop of timber is cut. Fish and shellfish can be overharvested, and farmland can be damaged or ruined by poor farming methods.

Resource Conservation and Recovery Act

The Resource Conservation and Recovery Act is the U.S. law that regulates solid waste disposal. It was passed by Congress in 1976 and has been strengthened several times since then. The law includes rules for landfills, recycling, and interstate garbage disposal.

Runoff

Runoff is rainwater or melted snow that is not absorbed into the soil. Instead, it trickles or pours across the earth's surface.

Lands with thick plant cover usually absorb

rainwater well, with little runoff. Land that has been paved, plowed, or logged absorbs less water and produces more runoff. There is also more runoff from sloping land than from flat land.

Runoff from farmland or timberland causes erosion and can carry large amounts of soil with it. This makes the land less fertile and pollutes nearby streams and rivers with mud. Runoff from farms and lawns may also pollute streams with fertilizers and pesticides.

S

Sahel (see DESERTIFICATION)

Salination

Fresh water has tiny amounts of salts dissolved in it. These salts are left behind when the water evaporates. This process is known as salination. When farmland is irrigated, the salts can gradually build up to levels that harm plant growth.

Salination can be controlled or avoided with careful irrigation management. Lands that become too salty can be flushed with large quantities of fresh water, for example. But unless care is taken, irrigated farmland can become barren salt flats.

Salt Marsh

A salt marsh is a tidal wetland. It is flooded with salt water at each high tide and left dry at each low tide. Plants and animals must be specially adapted to live in such conditions.

Salt marshes are very rich and productive environments. They are a breeding ground for fish, crabs, shrimp, and many other species. The flow of water brings nutrients to the marsh grasses. The plant roots and stems protect small animals. And the plants are a rich food source for the animals of the marsh. Marshes also protect inland areas from the waves and tides that come with heavy storms.

People make use of the marsh, too. Marsh grasses can be cut for livestock feed, known as salt hay. And of course, we eat the crabs, clams, shrimp, and fish that depend on the marsh for their rapid growth.

171

Unfortunately, people have only recently begun to understand the great value of marshland. Many marshes have been filled in or drained and then used for housing development, recreation, or even landfills.

Sanitary Sewer

Sanitary sewers are the underground pipelines that carry away the wastewater from toilets, sinks, bathtubs, and washing machines. Ordinarily, this wastewater is piped through the sewers to a wastewater treatment plant. There, it is treated to remove solids and nutrients and to kill germs before being returned to the environment (*see* SEPTIC SYSTEM, WASTEWATER TREATMENT).

Saprophyte

Saprophytes are fungi and a few unusual plants that get nutrients from dead plant and animal matter. Unlike green plants, saprophytes don't produce their own food through photosynthesis. Saprophytes play an important part in the food web as decomposers. They help break down dead plants and animals and return their nutrients to the soil.

Savanna

Savanna is tropical grassland, with scattered clusters of shrubs and trees. It is one of the earth's major biomes.

Savannas receive about 30 to 60 inches of rainfall a year. They have a long yearly dry season. During these annual droughts, fires sweep across the plains. These fires maintain the grassland and prevent the development of forests.

The world's largest savannas are in Africa. Many large mammals, including lions, elephants, hyenas, giraffes, antelopes, and zebras live in the African savanna. There are also savannas in South America and Australia.

Scavenger

A scavenger is an animal that eats the remains of dead plants or animals. Vultures are scavengers. They don't hunt and kill prey. They eat animals that have been killed by predators or that have died from other causes.

Other scavengers include crabs, beetles, ravens, termites, and jackals. Some animals, such as coyotes and hyenas, are both predators and scavengers. They will either hunt prey or eat animals that have already died.

Scavengers play an important part in any ecosystem. They begin the process of digesting dead animal matter and returning its nutrients to the soil.

Scrubber

A scrubber is an air pollution control device. It removes sulfur dioxide and other polluting gases from the exhausts of industrial smokestacks, such as those of coal- and oil-burning power plants. Scrubbers aren't used in home furnaces and chimneys.

Some scrubbers work by spraying a fine mist of water through the exhaust smoke. Others bubble the exhaust gases through a water tank. In either case, the pollutants dissolve in the water. The polluted water is then collected and treated. Meanwhile, the exhaust that continues to pour out of the stack is much cleaner.

Secondary Consumer (*see* CARNIVORE, CONSUMER, PREDATOR)

Sediment

Sediment is any material that settles to the bottom of a lake, river, or ocean. The sediment at the bottom of the ocean, for example, includes dead organisms, dust from the air, soil eroded from the continents, and chemical solids. Sediments build up slowly, year after year, in any body of water.

Over many thousands of years, sediment forms sedimentary rock. Fossil remains of plants and animals, including fossil fuels such as coal and petroleum, are often found in sedimentary rock. Scientists study these ancient layers of sediment to learn about events from the earth's distant past.

Selective Cutting

Selective cutting is a logging method in which only some trees are cut from a woodland. Loggers cut trees that are the right size and have the most value. Other trees are left standing. These reseed the sections that have been cut. When a woodland is thinned by selective cutting, the remaining trees get more sunlight and grow faster.

The remaining trees also protect the soil. Their roots prevent the erosion that happens when an entire woodland is clear-cut. Selective cutting is slower and more expensive than clear-cutting, but it is more effective in protecting the woodland environment (*see* FORESTRY, CLEAR-CUTTING).

Septic System

Septic means containing bacteria. A septic system is

used to treat household wastewater from toilets, sinks, tubs, and washing machines. Wastewater is piped into an underground septic tank. There, solids settle out and bacteria help digest the wastes. Liquid from the septic system flows through a series of pipes into an underground gravel bed, called a drainfield. The gravel helps to filter the wastewater as it slowly trickles into the surrounding soil.

Septic systems can be used where the soil is absorbent and where homes are not too close together. Cities and large suburban areas must use centralized sewers and wastewater treatment plants instead of individual septic systems. If septic systems are not installed and maintained correctly, they can pollute groundwater, wells, or surface streams. Septic tanks must be pumped regularly to prevent solids from clogging the drainfield.

Sewage Treatment (*see* WASTEWATER TREATMENT)

Sewer (*see* SANITARY SEWER, STORM SEWER)

Skin Cancer

Skin cancer refers to a group of diseases in which tumors grow on the skin. Some forms of skin cancer are minor and easily treated. Others are much more serious and often fatal.

Skin cancer has a number of causes. One of the most common is overexposure to the sun's ultraviolet rays. Some ultraviolet radiation is filtered out by the ozone layer in the earth's atmosphere. Because the ozone layer has been damaged in recent years, scientists expect the number of skin cancers to increase. Sunblocking lotions, which block the effects of ultraviolet radiation, reduce the risk of skin cancer.

Slash-and-Burn Agriculture

Slash-and-burn agriculture is a farming method widely practiced in tropical regions. A section of rain forest is cut down, or slashed. The wood is sold, and the remaining vegetation is simply burned. The newly cleared land is then planted with crops.

However, most of the nutrients in the rain forest are stored in the plants themselves. When they are removed, the remaining soil is poor. It can support a productive farm for only a few years. Then the farmers must move on and cut down a new section of forest.

This form of farming has been practiced by native peoples on small plots for thousands of years. As long as slash-and-burn plots are small and widely spaced, the rain forest can slowly recover after the farmers have moved on. But when large areas of forest are cut down for timber and ranchland, slash-and-burn agriculture is both wasteful and environmentally destructive. Rare species of plants and animals lose their habitat, and the soil is robbed of nutrients so that it becomes very difficult to restore the rain forest after the ground is no longer productive as farmland.

Sludge

Sludge is the solid waste that is left at the end of the wastewater treatment process. Sludge is a thick, dark, pasty material rich in plant nutrients. Some cities and towns dispose of sludge by spreading it on farmland or by selling it as fertilizer. One of the first cities to

176

recycle sludge in this way was Milwaukee, Wisconsin. Milwaukee sold its sludge fertilizer under the name Mil-Organite. Other cities simply bury sludge in landfills.

Sludge is treated so that disease-causing germs have been destroyed. But if the original wastewater contained industrial pollutants, those poisons may remain even after treatment. Sludge that contains heavy metals or other poisons must be handled as toxic waste and cannot be spread on fields.

Smog

The word *smog* is a combination of the words *smoke* and *fog*. Smog is a form of air pollution that often forms a brownish haze over modern cities. It is a mixture of pollutants, including hydrocarbons and nitrogen and sulfur oxides. Sunlight striking the chemicals in the air makes the pollution worse. It produces ozone, another irritating pollutant. Because of this effect, the complete name for this pollution is photochemical smog (photo means light).

Smog irritates the breathing passages of people and animals. It even damages steel and stone. In some cities, smog has become so bad at times that it has killed people who suffered from heart and lung diseases. Smog is at its worst in cities that lie in a valley surrounded by mountains. The mountains can hold the air in the valley for days, while the exhaust gases from cars and smokestacks build up. Los Angeles, Mexico City, and Santiago, Chile, all suffer from this problem. Cities with severe smog may have to reduce traffic or shut down industries when the smog reaches high levels.

Smokestack

A smokestack is one of the earliest pollution control

devices. It is a tall chimney that carries the industrial exhaust gases high into the air. Winds carry the gases away from the area. The pollution is diluted in the atmosphere, so it does less harm.

Modern smokestacks can be fitted with other pollution control devices—scrubbers and electrostatic precipitators—that remove many of the pollutants before the gases escape into the air.

Soil

Soil is the surface layer that covers much of the earth. It is made of fine particles of sand, clay, pebbles, and decayed plant and animal matter. Soil gives plant roots a place to take hold. It provides mineral nutrients for plant growth, and it holds the rainwater that plants also need. Many animals make their homes in the soil. The soil is also home to fungi and bacteria.

Soil varies widely from place to place in depth, in nutrient content, and in the ability to hold water. The soil in some regions—like the midwestern United States—is rich and fertile. In other regions, such as the rocky hills of northern New England, the soil is much thinner and poorer.

Valuable soil can be lost to erosion or poor farming practices. Planting the same crops year after year robs the soil of its nutrients (*see* MONOCROPPING). And years of irrigation can add salts to the soil, stunting plant growth (*see* SALINATION).

Solar Energy

Solar energy is the energy the earth receives from the sun. Almost all the energy coming into the earth's environment is solar energy. And almost every energy resource people use comes from solar radiation, either directly or indirectly.

The sun is the energy source for all our agriculture. It provides the energy that plants use for photosynthesis. It's the source for the heat released when wood is burned. Oil, natural gas, and coal are solar energy stored in the fossil remains of plants and animals. Wind energy, the energy of ocean waves, and the heat in the water and air are all generated by the energy of the sun.

Even hydroelectric power is driven by the sun's energy. Solar energy evaporates water from the earth's surface; winds then carry the water elsewhere to fall as rain that feeds our planet's rivers.

Solar energy can be changed to electrical energy with solar cells. Many homes and offices are heated directly with solar energy.

Of all the commonly used energy sources, the only ones that don't come from the sun are nuclear, tidal, and geothermal energy.

These solar collectors at a power plant in California use thousands of solar cells to convert the energy of the sun into electricity.

179

Solid Waste

Solid waste is what is commonly known as trash or garbage. Garbage is wet kitchen waste, the waste that results from food preparation. Trash is nontoxic, dry household waste, which can include paper, plastics, metals, leaves, and twigs. Solid waste is produced in both homes and the workplace. According to the Environmental Protection Agency, the average U.S. citizen produces about 4 pounds of solid waste a day, or almost 1,500 pounds a year. Other studies say U.S. citizens produce as much as 1,800 pounds per year. About one third of all this waste is packaging.

Some 40 percent of our solid waste is paper—newspapers alone make up 12 to 18 percent. Yard wastes—grass clippings, leaves, and branches—contribute about 18 percent. Plastics make up 8 percent and metals another 8 percent. Glass and food wastes each make up about 7 percent. The remaining wastes include cloth, wood, and construction debris. Polystyrene foam (Styrofoam) makes up less than 1 percent of solid wastes; disposable diapers, about 1.2 percent.

Most solid waste in the United States is disposed of in landfills. Some is burned in incinerators. Recycling can reduce the amount of solid waste that we throw away.

Species

A species is one particular kind of organism. Ordinarily, members of a species reproduce only with one another. The characteristics of the species are passed on from one generation to the next. Over many generations, a species can evolve (change) as it adapts to the conditions in its environment.

Standard of Living

The standard of living is a general measure of how well people live. It includes food, housing, clothing, medical care, and other goods and services that people want or need. Industrialized countries such as the United States, Japan, and the nations of Europe have the world's highest standards of living. Most people in these countries have more goods than they need to live. People in much of Africa and Asia have much lower standards of living. Many people in these regions have just enough food, clothing, and shelter to survive.

A country's standard of living can be measured by its gross national product (GNP). The GNP measures the money value of all the goods and services a country produces. The world's wealth is unevenly distributed, so GNPs vary widely from country to country. Switzerland has the world's highest per capita GNP—about $30,000 per person. The U.S. GNP is about $21,000 per person. Compare that with some of the world's poorest nations: The GNP of Bangladesh is $180 per person; that of Ethiopia is $120 per person.

A high standard of living is much more comfortable and pleasant, of course. But it has a high environmental cost: A high standard of living uses up the planet's renewable and nonrenewable raw materials at a fast rate. For example, the average U.S. citizen uses 76 times more energy than a person in Bangladesh.

Storm Sewer

Storm sewers are underground pipes that carry rainwater away from city streets. In most cases, runoff from storm sewers simply flows into the nearest river or lake. Any trash or pollutant washed or poured down the drain of a storm sewer goes directly into the environment. Dumping wastes such as motor oil, antifreeze, paint thinner, and other chemicals down storm drains causes water pollution.

A few cities with older sewer systems combine storm sewers with their sanitary sewer systems. Runoff from rainfall is treated along with other wastewater at the wastewater treatment plant. However, heavy rains may cause the treatment plant to overflow. When this happens, untreated sewage pours into the nearest river.

Storm Surge

Storm surge is the extra height and power of ocean waves driven by hurricanes and other oceanic storms. Much of the damage done by a hurricane is caused by its storm surge. Storm waves damage or flood buildings and roadways built too near the shore.

Salt marshes and barrier islands, if they are left undeveloped, absorb much of the energy of a storm surge and protect whatever is built behind them.

Stress

Stress is anything in an organism's environment that makes life more difficult. For example, a shortage of food or water creates a stress on an animal. So do unusual changes in climate or competition from other species.

Species must adapt to stress in order to survive. Those individuals who are best able to survive stresses will, of course, be most likely to have offspring. In this way, species evolve and adapt to a changing environment.

182

Strip-Mining

Strip-mining is a method of getting coal and mineral ores from the earth. In strip-mining, layers of surface soil and rock are stripped away until the minerals are uncovered. The minerals are then removed for processing. When minerals are near the surface, strip-mining is the least expensive way to mine them. Coal is the resource most often mined this way.

Strip-mining destroys the environment. In the past, mining companies simply abandoned an area after the minerals were removed. This left an eroding wasteland of bare rock and soil. U.S. law now requires mining companies to restore an area once strip-mining is completed. The land must be reclaimed and replanted. Nevertheless, it takes many years before this reclaimed land returns to near-natural conditions (*see* MINING).

Styrofoam (*see* POLYSTYRENE FOAM)

Subsoil

Subsoil is the layer of soil that lies beneath the topsoil. Subsoil is less fertile than topsoil because it contains less organic matter and fewer nutrients. When top-soil erodes away, leaving only subsoil, plants grow poorly.

Succession

Succession is a regular, orderly pattern of change and growth that an ecosystem goes through. Succession begins when the ecosystem is disturbed, perhaps by fire or agriculture. A succession might start on a barrier island swept clean by storm, on chaparral or

grassland after a fire, or on a new volcanic lava field. Succession is completed when the area becomes a climax, or mature, ecosystem. In a salt marsh, this process could take just a few years. For a forest ecosystem, a complete succession could take centuries.

Suppose a field in the eastern United States is abandoned and left to grow undisturbed. It first is taken over by annual grasses and low-growing weeds. Later, blackberries and perennial grasses dominate the habitat. Gradually, the field is colonized by shrubs and pine seedlings. The pines grow taller, shading out the smaller plants. Eventually, oak, hickory, and other hardwoods replace the shorter-lived pines. After many years, the once-bare field becomes a climax deciduous forest. If the woodland were to be destroyed by a forest fire, the whole process would begin once again. Most woodlands in the eastern United States were once cleared for agriculture and have gone through just such a process of succession.

Sulfur Dioxide

Sulfur dioxide is a poisonous gas produced when sulfur-containing fuels are burned. The chemical formula for sulfur dioxide is SO_2. Both coal and petroleum contain sulfur in varying amounts. When these fuels burn, sulfur dioxide is formed.

Sulfur dioxide is a serious air pollutant. As a gas, it is irritating and poisonous to breathe. In the air it combines with water vapor to form sulfuric acid. In this form, it is the main cause of acid rain. The sulfuric acid in acid rain harms plants and animals and even eats away the paint and stone of buildings.

Superfund

The Superfund was started by the U.S. Congress in 1980 in a law called the Comprehensive Environmental Response, Compensation and Liability Act. This law set aside $1.6 billion to clean up the worst toxic waste sites in the country—called the National Priority List (NPL).

Several times since 1980, Congress has added more money to the fund. Taxes on chemical companies provide most of the money for the Superfund. In addition, when companies pay fines for polluting, that money may go into the fund. Superfund money is also used for research into the best ways to clean up toxic wastes and to bring those who were responsible for toxic dumping to justice.

Since 1980, more than 1,200 toxic waste sites have been placed on the Superfund list. They are the worst of more than 32,000 toxic waste sites that have been found around the country. Even more of such sites are certain to be discovered.

By 1992, cleanup had been completed on only 64 NPL waste sites. A complete cleanup of NPL sites across the United States could cost more than $1 trillion, far more than is now available.

Survival of the Fittest (*see* EVOLUTION)

Sustainable Development (*see* DEVELOPMENT)

Sustainable Yield (*see* MAXIMUM SUSTAINABLE YIELD)

Swamp

A swamp is a wetland in which trees are the dominant plants. There are both freshwater and saltwater swamps. Saltwater swamps featuring tangled mangrove trees are common on tropical and semitropical coastlines, including the coast of southern Florida. Tall stands of cypress trees dominate the freshwater swamps of the southeastern United States.

Symbiosis

Symbiosis means living together. In a symbiotic relationship, two different creatures live together, and both gain something from the association. This relationship is also called mutualism. True symbiotic relationships are rare in nature.

A lichen is one example of a symbiotic relationship. It is a fungus and an alga living together. The alga, a green plant, produces food for the fungus by means of photosynthesis. The fungus provides support and body structure for the alga. Neither species can live without the other.

Another example of a symbiotic relationship is the oxpecker bird and the rhinoceros. The oxpecker removes insect pests from the rhino and alerts the large animal to danger. In return, the bird gets a steady supply of food.

Synergism

Sometimes the combined effect of two different chemicals is much greater than would be expected from just adding the effects of each substance together. This is

186

known as synergism or a synergistic effect. Synergism occurs with drugs and with some environmental hazards.

Cigarette smoke and asbestos are both cancer-causing substances. They also work synergistically. Someone who has been exposed to asbestos dust and who also smokes has a much greater risk of developing lung cancer, because the two carcinogens work together synergistically.

Smog is another example of synergism. When the pollutants in smog mix together, the result is much worse than would be expected just from the levels of the individual pollutants.

Synfuels/Synthetic Fuels

Synthetic means human-made or artificial. Synthetic fuels are liquid or gaseous fuels made from coal or biomass (biological materials such as corn, sawdust, or garbage). These raw materials are changed to oil-like liquids or gases that can be burned in furnaces or engines. For example, coal can be converted into a mixture of hydrogen, methane, and carbon monoxide, which can be burned as fuel. Alcohol fuels can be produced from wood chips, sawdust, or grains.

Synthetic fuels are a possible replacement for shrinking supplies of oil and natural gas. However, much of the synthetic fuel industry is still in the experimental stage.

T

Taiga

Taiga is northern coniferous forest. It is one of the world's major biomes. It is also known as boreal forest. The taiga covers northern regions of Europe, Asia, and North America. Its climate is harsh and cold, with a short growing season. The taiga receives about 25 inches of rainfall per year.

There is little diversity of species in the taiga. The most common trees are spruce and fir, both evergreens. In areas cleared by fire, birch and aspens grow, along with lower-growing shrubs. Typical animal species include hares, mice, ducks, lemmings, moose, lynx, and wolves.

Temperate Coniferous Forests

The temperate coniferous forest is one of the earth's major biomes. It has a cool, seasonal climate, with warm summers and long, cold winters. Rainfall is plentiful and is distributed fairly evenly throughout the year.

Temperate coniferous forest is found in northern New England, southern Canada, and the Pacific Northwest. It is also found in northern Europe and sections of northern Asia. The dominant trees of this biome are conifers such as hemlock, juniper, spruce, and fir, often mixed with deciduous trees such as maple and birch. Common animals include moose, elk, squirrels and chipmunks, owls, bluejays, and chickadees.

Temperate Deciduous Forest

The temperate deciduous forest is one of the earth's

major biomes. It has a moderate, seasonal climate, with hot summers and cool winters. Rainfall averages between 30 and 60 inches per year and is distributed fairly evenly throughout the year.

Temperate deciduous forest is the biome that covers most of the eastern United States. It also includes most of Europe and large sections of eastern China and eastern Australia. Much of these regions are now cleared of forest and used for agriculture or urban development.

The dominant trees in this biome are deciduous: They lose their leaves each fall and grow them again each spring. In the United States, the most common species of trees include oak, hickory, beech, maple, and poplar. Typical animals of this biome include squirrels, deer, wild turkeys, foxes, raccoons, and black bears.

Temperate Rain Forest

The temperate rain forest is one of the earth's smaller biomes. It is sometimes known as cloud forest. Temperate rain forest is found in limited areas where rainfall is heavy but temperatures are moderate or cool. There are sections of temperate rain forest in the Olympic Peninsula of Washington State, along the west coast of British Columbia and Alaska, and in tropical mountain regions.

The temperate rain forest has lush plant growth, with stands of large firs or other trees. Ferns and mosses grow in the damp shade beneath these trees. There are far fewer different species of plants and animals in the temperate rain forest than there are in the tropical rain forest.

Temperature Inversion

A temperature inversion is a climate pattern in which

a layer of warm air lies above a layer of cooler air near the earth's surface. The two layers of air stay separated. The warmer air above keeps the pocket of cooler air trapped in one place for a few hours, or for days or even weeks.

A temperature inversion also traps smoke, smog, and other pollutants in the lower, cooler layer of air. The pollutants can't blow away into the surrounding atmosphere as they ordinarily do. Temperature inversions are worst in winter, when the earth's surface is cool. They can raise air pollution to life-threatening levels in some cities.

Warm Air

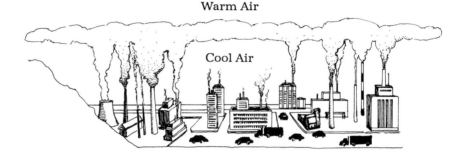

Cool Air

Thermal Pollution

Thermal pollution occurs when human activities raise the temperature in the environment higher than it normally would be. Factories and power plants are often built beside rivers or lakes to use water as a coolant. When the water is returned to the river or lake, it is unnaturally warm.

This warmer water can cause unusually rapid plant growth. It can also kill animals or disrupt their regular life cycles or migration habits. In wintertime, heat can draw animals away from their normal habitat. Predators may become dependent on prey drawn to the warmer area.

In cities, the heat from cars, buildings, and factories causes local air temperatures to be several degrees warmer than the surrounding countryside. This process can also be considered a form of thermal pollution.

Thermocline

Cold water is denser than warm water and the two don't mix easily. Cold water sinks to the bottom of a pond, lake, or ocean, while the surface is warmed by the sun. The place where the layers meet is called a thermocline.

Thermoclines are very noticeable on warm summer days. In the wintertime, thermoclines may disappear as an entire body of water becomes cold. Some organisms prefer to live in the warm waters above a thermocline; others remain in the cooler waters below it. And some organisms migrate between the two layers to search for food or shelter.

Thermoregulation

In most environments, temperatures vary widely from hot to cold. But animals must keep their body temperatures within a much narrower range to survive. Thermoregulation is the ability of an animal to keep its body temperature within a safe range.

Animals use many different methods to thermoregulate. Mammals and birds are "warm-blooded." They burn food as fuel to keep their bodies at a constant temperature. In colder weather, these animals need more food to survive. People get rid of excess body heat by sweating. As the sweat evaporates, our bodies get cooler. Other animals lose extra heat by opening their mouths and panting.

The body temperature of "cold-blooded" animals varies with the temperature of the environment. When the air or water temperature is cool, so is the animal. Body processes and movements slow down as the animal's body cools. Cold-blooded animals

191

thermoregulate by absorbing heat from their environment to warm up. They move to cooler locations when they get too hot. For example, lizards and snakes bask in the sun to warm their bodies. They cool themselves by moving to the shade or water, or crawling underground.

Threatened Species

According to the Endangered Species Act of 1973, a threatened species is any creature "likely to become endangered in the foreseeable future" in all or a portion of its habitat. Threatened species are not in as much trouble as endangered species, but they could soon be in danger of extinction.

Three Mile Island

Three Mile Island, Pennsylvania, is the location of a nuclear power plant. In 1979, there was a serious accident in its reactor, the worst in U.S. history. After a series of mistakes and equipment failures, the core of the reactor was destroyed. Some radioactive gas was released into the air. Fortunately, the core did not "melt down" through the floor of the reactor. Most of the radioactive material was held inside the reactor building.

By the early 1990s, $1 billion had been spent on cleaning up the radioactive waste left by the accident. And the cleanup had not been completed. Some of the cleanup was done by remote control, to protect workers from radiation poisoning. The accident at Three Mile Island helped convince U.S. power companies not to order new nuclear reactors.

Tidal Power

Tidal power is electricity generated by the rise and

fall of ocean tides. To generate electricity, water is trapped behind a dam as the tide rises. Then, when the tide falls, the water is released. As it flows back toward the ocean, it runs through turbines that turn electrical generators. When the tide begins to rise again, water builds up on the other side of the dam. It then flows through the turbines in the other direction, generating electricity once again.

The world's first tidal power plant was built across the Rance River in France in 1966. The plant takes advantage of tidal differences of 40 feet or more in the English Channel.

Tidal power is only practical where there are large differences between high and low tides. And it can only generate power during part of each day. The advantage of tidal power is that it burns no fuel, creates no pollution, and relies on a constantly renewable source of energy.

Times Beach

Times Beach is a small town near St. Louis, Missouri. It was the site of a famous environmental disaster in the early 1980s.

Times Beach was polluted with dioxins when its roads were accidentally sprayed with contaminated oil. In 1983, the government spent $36 million to buy the entire town and resettle all its citizens. Most of the money came from the Superfund set up by Congress to clean up the environment.

Topsoil

Topsoil is the upper layer of the soil. It is usually dark and rich in humus (decayed plant material) and plant nutrients. It has more nutrients than the layers of subsoil below it. Agriculture depends on this valuable natural resource.

Topsoil builds up over many years as dead plant and animal material decays and enriches it. It can be lost when wind or water erodes it. Land that has been plowed, strip-mined, or cleared of trees is in the greatest danger of losing topsoil to erosion.

Toxic Waste

Toxic waste is any poisonous by-product of human activities. Many industries produce toxic wastes. For example, poisonous dioxins are made as a by-product of manufacturing herbicides and paper.

Many industrial products are poisonous to humans and wildlife. So are ordinary household products such as fuels, paints, cleaners, and pesticides. Whenever these materials are thrown away, they become toxic waste.

Toxic wastes are often difficult and expensive to handle. That tempts some people to save money by dumping them illegally. Unless they are disposed of properly, toxic wastes can do great harm to humans, plants, and animals.

Toxin

A toxin is any poison. Many plants and animals produce toxins naturally, for defense. For example, rattlesnakes use a toxin to capture prey and protect themselves from predators. Poison ivy has a toxic oil that gives people a rash. Some plants and fungi produce toxins that are deadly to humans if eaten even in small amounts.

Toxins are also manufactured by people. Insecticides, which are poisonous to insects, are one example. Many toxins are made as by-products of industrial processes. For instance, sulfur dioxide is a toxic gas released when coal or fuel oil is burned.

Transect

A transect is a systematic survey of a section of the environment. It is a way of learning about an ecosystem by examining carefully chosen sample areas in it.

In a transect, equal-size areas are marked off at regular distances along a survey line. For example, ecologists conducting a marsh transect might mark off areas of 1 square meter every 10 meters. They would then study the living and nonliving factors they find in each marked area and compare the areas they have studied.

Tropical Rain Forest

The tropical rain forest is one of the earth's major biomes. Tropical rain forests have year-round hot temperatures and annual rainfalls of 80 inches or more. Some rain forests get as much as 400 inches of rain. Tropical rain forests are found in Central and South America, central Africa, Southeast Asia, Australia, and Indonesia. Smaller regions of rain forest are located on some tropical islands, including Hawaii.

Because of the heat and moisture, plants in the rain forest grow thickly and dead material decays rapidly. The soil in most rain forests is poor and thin. Nutrients in the ecosystem are taken up quickly by the growing plants themselves.

Tropical rain forests have many more species living in them than any other biome. Scientists estimate that about half the world's species live in the rain forests. Many rain-forest species, both plants and animals, have yet to be found and classified by biologists. Some of these undiscovered species could become sources of new medicines or other products.

Large areas of the rain forest are being destroyed. The rain forest means economic opportunity to people in poor tropical nations. Often, it also means profits for distant corporations in industrialized nations. About 50 million acres of rain forest are being cut down for timber, farmland, and grazing land each year.

Because most of the nutrients are stored in the plants themselves, the cleared land is poor for farming. After a few years, the farmland is usually abandoned. But without the nutrients, the forest cannot regrow easily.

Many rain-forest species may become extinct because their habitat is being destroyed. Native peoples, who have lived in the rain forests for centuries, are also threatened. Environmental groups are now making special efforts to protect the world's remaining rain forests.

Tropism

A tropism is a tendency of a plant to grow either toward or away from something. For example, plants are phototropic. That means they grow toward light. Roots are geotropic—they grow down. Plant roots are also hydrotropic—they grow toward water. Some plants, especially climbing plants such as peas and grapes, are thigmotropic. That means they grow toward other things they touch.

Tropisms help plants survive. Phototropism helps a plant reach the sunlight it needs in order to grow. Geotropism and hydrotropism help a plant's roots find water and nutrients.

Plants don't have muscles or nerves. Their movement is created by chemicals called hormones. The hormones speed up or slow down cell growth in different parts of the plant. The plant moves because the cells in different areas grow at different rates.

Tundra

Tundra is flat, treeless land in the northern regions of North America, Europe, and Asia. It is one of the earth's major biomes.

The tundra is not a very productive biome. It has very cold temperatures for most of the year and a very short growing season. Only the top few feet of soil thaw out each summer. Beneath that is a permanently frozen layer of subsoil called permafrost.

Plants common to the tundra include lichens, grasses, and low woody plants like willows and birches. Tundra animals include caribou, Arctic hare, foxes, wolves, mice, and lemmings. Large flocks of geese, ducks, and other birds migrate to the tundra during its short summer.

Because of the short growing season and underlying permafrost, the tundra is especially fragile. Any damage by human activity takes many years to heal.

Turtle Excluder

Endangered sea turtles are often swept up in the nets of shrimp boats. The turtles usually drown before the nets are brought to the surface. Many fish are also caught and killed in the shrimpers' nets.

A turtle excluder is a device placed in shrimp nets. It lets sea turtles and most fish escape through a trapdoor. The law now requires U.S. shrimp boats to use turtle excluders. Many shrimpers don't want to use the excluders because the devices reduce the size of their catches.

U

Ultraviolet (UV) Radiation

Ultraviolet radiation—also known as ultraviolet light—is a form of radiant energy. It is a part of sunlight, but it isn't visible to human eyes.

Ultraviolet light has more energy than visible light. It causes sunburn; in large doses, it is very harmful to life. It can cause blindness, severe burning, and skin cancer. Artificial sources of UV radiation are sometimes used to kill germs.

Fortunately, most of the UV radiation in sunlight is filtered out by the ozone layer in the earth's upper atmosphere. In recent years, the ozone layer has been damaged (*see* OZONE LAYER). This is a concern because a damaged ozone layer won't protect the earth from harmful UV radiation.

Underground Storage Tank

An underground storage tank is a large container for liquids buried below the surface of the ground. Such tanks are often used to store gasoline or other fuels. Most service stations have several of them beneath their gasoline pumps. Underground storage tanks are also used as temporary storage for hazardous waste. For example, the Hanford nuclear weapons plant in Washington State has millions of gallons of deadly radioactive waste stored in underground tanks.

Underground storage tanks can leak. Because they are buried out of sight, leaks may not be discovered for a long time. The World Resources Institute says there could be 10,000 leaking underground fuel tanks in the United States. Some of these tanks

199

have been abandoned. Some have even been lost. The leaks contaminate the soil and groundwater. Underground tanks must be built of materials that won't develop leaks easily, and they must be checked regularly to avoid such problems.

Upwelling

Upwelling is an upward current in a lake or ocean. It brings cool, nutrient-rich waters from the depths to the water's surface.

Upwelling is caused when surface water cools. Water is most dense at 39°F (4°C). The cold, dense water on the surface sinks, and as it does, it pushes other water upward toward the surface. The upwelling carries dissolved minerals and nutrients from the bottom of the lake or ocean.

Upwelling is common in certain parts of the ocean. For example, the coasts of Peru and Ecuador usually have an upwelling current. Because of the nutrients in the current, these areas are rich in plankton, fish, and other marine life.

Uranium

Uranium is a radioactive metal. It is the heaviest chemical element that occurs naturally on earth. Uranium is used as fuel for nuclear reactors and nuclear weapons.

Uranium is a very hazardous material. As with other radioactive materials, exposure to uranium can cause burns, radiation sickness, and cancer.

Large amounts of uranium ore must be mined and processed to gather small amounts of this metal. The wastes from this mining—called tailings—are also an environmental hazard. They are slightly radioactive and also may leach acids into nearby streams and rivers.

Urban Decay

Urban decay is a social, political, and environmental problem in many U.S. cities. As cities spread outward into the suburbs, their central areas are often neglected. The inner city is the area with the oldest roads and buildings. Wealthier people may move to the suburbs, where the environment is more pleasant. Many of the people who remain in the city are poor, with fewer resources and less political power. Meanwhile, the city is still the cultural and business center for the region. To keep up services, taxes are often much higher in the city— another reason for people to move to the suburbs.

As a result of these and other factors, the inner city begins to decay. Roads, bridges, and buildings need repair. Businesses, factories, and offices move to the suburbs. Jobs leave the center city, so there is more unemployment. Crime increases. There are fewer resources to support schools, parks, recreation, and cultural events. In short, the city environment becomes less and less attractive to residents.

Urban Renewal

Urban renewal is an attempt to fix urban decay. In earlier years, urban renewal meant tearing down large areas of slum dwellings and replacing them with new housing. This kind of urban renewal didn't work well, because it destroyed neighborhoods.

Urban renewal now has a broader meaning. It can include building new housing or repairing older homes. Urban renewal can also include the creation

201

of parks and recreational facilities, repair of streets, and the creation of new businesses and industries for city residents.

Urban Sprawl

As populations increase, cities spread farther into the surrounding countryside. This is known as urban sprawl. Urban sprawl depends on the automobile. It features broad highways radiating out from the center city, with malls and shopping centers, and large sections of single-family homes on small plots of land.

In most cases, urban sprawl happens with little planning. Urban sprawl uses land inefficiently. It makes people spend large amounts of energy and time to get to work, shopping, school, or recreation. As a city sprawls outward, the central areas often become poor and neglected (*see* URBAN DECAY).

UV Light (*see* ULTRAVIOLET RADIATION)

V

Vapor Recovery System

Liquid gasoline evaporates quickly. Fumes from gasoline stations contribute to air pollution. A vapor recovery system is a pollution control device. It is placed on the nozzles of gasoline pumps. As gasoline flows into a car's gas tank, the recovery system captures the vapor and draws it back into the station's storage tanks. Capturing the fumes also conserves fuel.

Gas stations in some cities already have vapor recovery systems on their pumps. As clean air laws become stricter, more and more gasoline stations will have to use them.

Virgin Forest (*see* OLD GROWTH FOREST)

Virus

A virus is the smallest living thing known. Scientists still disagree about whether a virus is actually alive. Viruses are so small they can only be seen through an electron microscope. They can be found in fresh and salt water and in the soil by the billions.

Viruses have an outer shell made of protein, surrounding an inner core of DNA. This inner core contains the directions needed for the virus to reproduce. Viruses cannot grow or reproduce on their own. Instead, a virus infects a living cell. It then uses the cell's own material to produce copies of itself. In the process, the cell is destroyed.

Viruses cause many human diseases, from the common cold to measles and chicken pox to AIDS. Some viruses infect plants or animals. There are even viruses that specialize in attacking bacteria.

203

Because they are so small, viruses are difficult to study. Much more remains to be learned about the place of viruses in the environment.

Vitrification

Vitrification is a process in which dangerous toxic or radioactive wastes are incorporated into glass before being buried deep in the earth. Sealing the waste into glass immobilizes it, preventing it from escaping into the environment. Vitrification is likely to be used to dispose of the deadly wastes left over from the production of nuclear weapons.

Volcanic Eruption

A volcanic eruption can have huge effects on the environment. The flows of molten lava and ash change the landscape and kill plants and wildlife. Eruptions also have positive results: Volcanic ash produces very fertile soil, for example.

In 1980, Mount St. Helens in Washington State exploded so violently that an entire mountainside was destroyed, along with all the trees and animal life on it. Sixty people were killed in the explosion, and the entire region was covered with a thick layer of volcanic ash.

The 1991 eruption of Mount Pinatubo in the Philippines was the largest of the 20th century. About 200,000 people were forced to leave their homes. The eruption threw huge amounts of volcanic material into the air, creating a layer of dust and smoke in the upper atmosphere. Scientists believe that this layer made the earth's climate at least one degree cooler during the following year.

W

War

War destroys human lives. And no war can be fought without terrible environmental damage.

For example, in the Persian Gulf War between Iraq and UN forces in 1991, about 600 oil wells were set afire. They polluted the air with smoke, fumes, and acid rain. Huge pools of oil spread across the desert, poisoning the land and water supplies and killing wildlife. The largest oil spill in history—up to 4 million barrels—spread across the Persian Gulf itself, killing fish, seabirds, and other marine creatures.

Large stretches of desert were dug up and filled with explosive mines. The bombing and shelling tore apart the earth's surface. In the fragile desert environment, this damage will take many years to heal.

Throughout history, armies have devastated the land in order to weaken or punish the enemy. In the 20th century, chemical and biological weapons—poison gases, herbicides, and deadly bacteria and viruses—have also become part of the modern military arsenal (see BIOLOGICAL WARFARE).

Wastewater

Wastewater is the used water that flows from homes and industries, along with the human and industrial wastes it contains. Household wastewater comes from flushed toilets, sinks, tubs, washing machines, and dishwashers. Wastewater from washing, called gray water, is sometimes treated separately from sewage that contains human wastes.

Factories use large amounts of water for many different processes. Industrial wastewater may contain a variety of chemicals, including toxic chemicals.

205

More than 95 percent of all sewage produced in the United States receives some form of treatment (*see* next entry). But some human wastes are still flushed directly into the nation's streams and rivers without any treatment at all.

Wastewater Treatment

Sewage, or wastewater, contains bacteria, plant nutrients, and chemicals that damage the environment if they are released directly into it. Wastewater treatment is the process that removes these pollutants.

Most municipal (city and town) wastewater treatment is done in three stages:

- **Pretreatment.** First, the sewage passes through screens to remove large pieces of debris—such as wood, rags, and plastics—that would clog the pipes of the treatment plant. The wastewater is then held in a settling tank to remove grit, sand, and silt. No human wastes or bacteria are removed at this stage.

- **Primary treatment.** In this step, the wastewater moves to sludge settling tanks. Here, 30 to 50 percent of the solids, including human waste, settle to the bottom of the tank. Chemicals are sometimes added to speed this process. Grease and oils float to the top and are removed. The material removed at this step is called raw sludge. More than 20 percent of U.S. treatment plants release the wastewater back into the environment after this stage.

- **Secondary treatment.** In this stage, the sewage is digested by billions of microscopic bacteria, protista, and fungi. The

206

wastewater is either trickled over beds of rocks and pebbles or stirred and aerated in large tanks. Either method gives the microscopic decomposers lots of oxygen to help them grow. After secondary treatment, 85 to 95 percent of the solids have settled out of the wastewater as sludge. However, dissolved nutrients—such as nitrates or phosphates—and chemical pollutants are still in the wastewater.

•**Tertiary treatment.** The best treatment plants use further, tertiary treatment. In this stage, some of the dissolved chemicals—either nutrients or toxins—are removed. This can be done with chemical treatments or with green plants in a marshlike sewage lagoon.

Before the wastewater is released back into a local river or stream, it is treated with chlorine to kill disease-causing bacteria. The sludge that settles out during primary and secondary treatment must also be treated. It is either composted or digested in tanks by anaerobic bacteria. At the end of this process, the treated sludge contains no harmful bacteria. It is spread on fields as fertilizer or buried in landfills. If sludge from industrial wastewater contains heavy metals or other poisons, it must be treated as toxic waste.

Many individual homes use septic systems to treat wastewater. (*see* SEPTIC SYSTEM).

Water

Water is a simple compound (H_2O) necessary for life on earth. Living cells are mostly water. In each cell, the chemicals necessary for life are dissolved in the water.

Creatures get water from the environment in different ways. Many simply drink. Some animals get all the water they need from the plants they eat. Smaller organisms absorb water directly through cell walls. Most plants absorb water, along with dissolved nutrients, through their roots. Desert plants and animals even rely on dew for their water supply.

Humans use water for drinking, cooking, and washing, and for agriculture and industry. Each day, U.S. homes use almost 200 gallons of water per person. Agriculture and industry use another 1,100 gallons per person each day. Each toilet flush uses 3 to 5 gallons. A bath takes 30 to 40 gallons; a shower, 20 to 30 gallons. Washing a load of clothes uses 20 to 30 gallons. Each gallon of water we use must eventually pass through a wastewater treatment system.

We get water from a variety of sources: lakes, rivers, springs and wells that tap underground aquifers, rainwater, and even desalination plants that make fresh water from seawater. Water is a renewable resource; rainfall replaces water that we use. But water resources can also be overused or polluted. Unsafe drinking water is a leading cause of disease and death in many of the world's poorer nations.

In some areas, such as the southwestern United States, water is scarce. It may be rationed during dry periods, and land development may also be restricted.

Water Cycle/Hydrologic Cycle

The water cycle is the path that water follows as it passes through the environment. The water cycle begins as rain falls. The rain runs across the land in streams and rivers or trickles into underground rivers known as aquifers. Plants and animals absorb some of this water and use it for their life functions. Eventually, most water runs into the world's oceans.

Solar energy evaporates water from the oceans,

rivers, and land. Water also evaporates from plant leaves into the air. The water vapor condenses in the cooler upper atmosphere and falls once again as rain, completing the cycle.

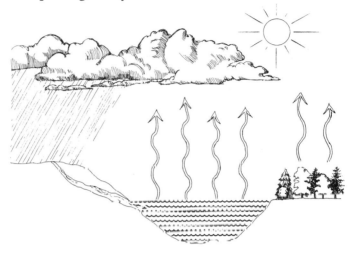

Water Pollution

Water pollution is anything that spoils the quality of streams, lakes, rivers, oceans, or groundwater. Water pollution comes from many sources. These include sewage, improperly treated wastewater, pesticides or fertilizers from farms, runoff from lawns or city streets, mud and silt eroded from plowed fields or construction sites, fluids from leaking automobiles or underground fuel tanks, household chemicals poured into city sewer systems, and even the waste heat from factories or power plants. Whenever people use a lake or river as a dump for wastes, water pollution results.

Some pollutants damage water by poisoning wildlife. Others, such as fertilizers, add nutrients that encourage rapid plant growth. This chokes the waterway and robs it of oxygen when the plants later die and decay.

209

Since all creatures need clean water to live, water pollution is a serious concern. Good sewer systems, complete wastewater treatment, contour plowing, forest preservation, regular inspection of storage tanks, water conservation, and proper disposal of household chemicals are just some of the ways that water pollution problems can be reduced.

Watershed

A watershed is the region of land drained by a particular stream or river. The Mississippi River watershed, for instance, drains about 1.25 million square miles—about one third of the entire United States. The Colorado River watershed covers about a quarter of a million square miles, including parts of Arizona, California, Colorado, Nevada, New Mexico, Utah, and Wyoming.

Because watersheds spread over such wide areas, pollution that runs into a stream in one place can affect ecosystems that are hundreds of miles away.

Water Table

The water table is the top surface of groundwater. As the amount of water in an aquifer increases or decreases, the water table rises or falls. If too much water is taken from an aquifer, rains will not be able to resupply it and bring the water table back to its original level.

Water Treatment

Many homes rely on individual wells for their fresh water supply. As long as these wells are unpolluted, the water is usually used without any treatment. Most cities and towns supply homes with water from a central source—a lake, river, or community wells.

Municipal water is usually treated to make sure it is clean and safe to drink.

Water goes through several steps in the treatment process. These include:

- **Filtration.** The water passes through fine screens to remove small particles.

- **Aeration.** Air is bubbled through the water, or the water is sprayed into the air. This removes dissolved gases that can give the water a bad taste. The oxygen also destroys chemical impurities in the water.

- **Chlorination.** Chlorine is added to kill disease-causing bacteria.

Wave Power

Wave power is electrical energy generated by the motion of ocean waves. Wave power is actually a form of solar energy. Ocean waves are driven by the action of the wind. Winds in turn are caused when regions of the land and water are heated unevenly by the sun.

Wave power is still experimental. Practical wave-powered generators are not yet in operation.

Weathering

Weathering is the slow wearing away of rock into fine particles of soil. Weathering is caused by erosion, chemical changes in the rock, and the actions of organisms such as lichens and plant roots.

Wetland

A wetland is an area of land that is covered with

water for at least a portion of the year. Marshes, swamps, and bogs are all wetlands.

Wetlands are often very productive areas. The plants and animals in a wetland are adapted to living in a specialized environment. Draining or filling a wetland completely changes the habitat and makes it impossible for wetland creatures to survive there (*see* BOG, MARSH, SWAMP).

Whales

Whales are large sea-dwelling mammals. There are at least 75 different species of whales in the world's oceans. Blue whales are the largest creatures ever to have lived on earth. They grow up to 100 feet long. Dolphins are the smallest member of the whale group. Whales are intelligent and can communicate with one another through sounds and songs.

Whales have suffered greatly at the hands of human hunters. In the first half of the 20th century, using modern ships and weapons, people killed whales by the hundreds of thousands. They were processed for meat, oil, and other products, such as glue, fertilizer, and pet food. All the commercially valuable species of whales were hunted so heavily that they are now endangered.

The International Whaling Commission was created in 1948. It set limits on the number of whales that could be caught. In 1985, a worldwide moratorium, or temporary halt, on commercial whaling began. Native peoples, such as the Eskimo, who traditionally depend on whales are allowed to continue hunting. Several countries—Japan, Iceland, Norway, and Russia—opposed the moratorium and have continued some whaling.

Wilderness

Wilderness is an area set aside by the government to

remain undisturbed by human activities. In a wilderness area, logging, construction, vehicles, and businesses are not allowed. In the United States, the Wilderness Preservation Society was established by Congress in 1964.

Since then, about 95 million acres—some 4 percent of U.S. lands—have been set aside as wilderness areas. More than half of that land is in Alaska. The Wilderness Society believes another 95 million acres of U.S. land could also qualify to be protected.

U.S. wilderness areas include mountain forests, swampland, desert, prairie, sections of salt marsh, and even a number of whitewater rivers.

Wildlife Refuge/Wildlife Sanctuary

A wildlife refuge or sanctuary is an area of protected habitat where plants and animals are left undisturbed to live and breed. As humans develop more land for their own uses, wildlife refuges become more important for the survival of other species.

Wind Power

Wind power is the generation of electricity from wind energy. The wind turns propellerlike blades set on tall towers. The propellers then turn electrical generators. Using wind power is not a new idea. The technology is already well developed. Farmers have used wind power to pump water and generate small amounts of electricity for many years.

The big advantage of wind power is that it relies on a renewable resource. Winds are created by solar energy. The earth heats and cools unevenly. The air above a warm part of the earth warms more quickly than the air above a cooler region. The warm air rises. Cooler air then rushes in to take its place, creating wind. As long as the sun heats the planet, there will be wind to run electrical generators.

However, wind power also has disadvantages. In many places, the winds don't blow regularly enough to supply reliable power. In general, coastal regions have the most dependable winds. Even there, the wind doesn't always have enough force to meet energy needs. So wind generators must be backed up with other power sources. People may also think the tall generators spoil the scenic value of a region.

Wind power at work. Rotating blades convert the energy of the wind to electrical power.

Zonation

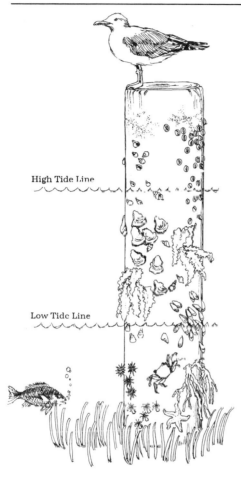

High Tide Line

Low Tide Line

Zonation is the division of water or land areas into different habitats. Each zone is populated by a characteristic group of living things.

Zonation can be clearly seen at any seacoast. The spray zone is populated by barnacles and periwinkle snails. Where the water covers the rocks at high tide, oysters grow, along with a few seaweeds such as bright green sea lettuce. Nearer the low tide line are blue mussels. Just below the low tide line live sea urchins, sea stars, and small fish. The animals of each zone live only in that specialized habitat.

Zonation is also easily seen on a mountain. As the elevation changes, so do the kinds of plants and animals that live on the mountainside.

Zoning

Zoning is a political process within a town or city that decides what kinds of development are allowed. Some sections of a community are zoned for business. Other areas may be zoned for industry, housing, or agriculture.

Each locality has its own zoning board—a group of community members who make zoning decisions. Developers who want to build new homes, businesses, or factories have to get permission from the zoning board first. If it is used well, zoning can help a community control and plan its development wisely.

Zooplankton

Plankton are the microscopic life that floats near the surface of the water in oceans or lakes. Some planktonic creatures are plants (*see* PHYTOPLANKTON). Others, known as zooplankton, are animals.

Some zooplankton are the larvae of creatures such as crabs, oysters, barnacles, clams, and shrimp. These will later leave the plankton as they grow larger and change form. Other animals spend their entire lives as specks of plankton, feeding on the other tiny creatures floating in the water.

ENVIRONMENTAL ORGANIZATIONS

The following are a number of national organizations that work toward protecting the environment.

Citizen's Clearinghouse for Hazardous Wastes, P.O. Box 6806, Falls Church, VA 22040, (703) 237-2249

The Cousteau Society, 870 Greenbrier Circle, Suite 402, Chesapeake, VA 23320, (804) 523-9335

Defenders of Wildlife, 1244 19th Street NW, Washington, DC 20036, (202) 659-9510

Earth First!, P.O. Box 5176, Missoula, MT 59806

Earth Island Institute, 300 Broadway, Suite 28, San Francisco, CA 94133, (415) 788-3666

Environmental Defense Fund, 257 Park Avenue, New York, NY 10010, (212) 505-2100

Friends of the Earth, 1025 Vermont Avenue NW, Suite 300, Washington, DC 20005, (202) 783-7400

Greenpeace International, 1436 U Street NW, Washington, DC 20009, (202) 462 1177

League of Conservation Voters, 1707 L Street NW, Washington, DC 20026, (202) 785-8683

National Audubon Society, 950 Third Avenue, New York, NY 10022, (212) 832-3200

National Wildlife Federation, 1400 16th Street NW, Washington, DC 20036, (202) 797-6800

Natural Resources Defense Council, 40 W. 20th Street, New York, NY 10011, (212) 727-2700

The Nature Conservancy, 1815 N. Lynn Street, Arlington, VA 22209, (703) 841-5300

Rainforest Action Network, 450 Sansome, Suite 700, San Francisco, CA 94111, (415) 398-4404

Sierra Club, 730 Polk Street, San Francisco, CA 94109, (415) 776-2211

Student Conservation Association, Box 550, Charlestown, NH 03603, (603) 543-1700

Student Environmental Action Coalition, P.O. Box 1168, Chapel Hill, NC 27514, (919) 967-4600

The Wilderness Society, 900 17th Street NW, Washington, DC 20006, (202) 833-2300

Wildlife Conservation International, c/o New York Zoological Society, Bronx, NY 10460, (718) 220-5155

World Wildlife Fund, 1250 24th Street NW, Washington, DC 20037, (202) 293-4800

Zero Population Growth, 1400 16th Street NW, Suite 320, Washington, DC 20036, (202) 332-2200

For a listing of other organizations, check the *Encyclopedia of Associations* in the reference section of your public library. There are also many local and regional organizations throughout the United States and the world.

FOR FURTHER READING

BOOKS FOR YOUNG PEOPLE

Bash, Barbara, *Tree of Life: The World of the African Baobab*, Sierra Club, 1989

Bloyd, Sunni, *Animal Rights*, Lucent, 1990

_____ , *Endangered Species*, Lucent, 1989

Burleigh, Robert, *A Man Named Thoreau*, Macmillan, 1985

Caduto, Michael J. and Joseph Bruchac, *Keepers of the Earth: Native American Stories and Environmental Activities for Children*, Fulcrum, 1988

Dorris, Michael, *Morning Girl*, Hyperion, 1992 (fiction)

Elkington, John et al., *Going Green: A Kid's Handbook to Saving the Planet*, Penguin, 1990

Facklam, Howard and Margery Facklam, *Plants: Extinction or Survival?*, Enslow, 1990

Fleisher, Paul, *Changing Our World: A Handbook for Young Activists*, Zephyr Press, 1993

Gallant, Roy A., *The Peopling of Planet Earth: Human Population Growth Through the Ages*, Macmillan, 1990

Gay, Kathlyn, *Garbage and Recycling*, Enslow, 1991

George, Jean Craighead, *The Missing 'Gator of Gumbo Limbo*, HarperTrophy, 1992 (fiction)

_____ , *My Side of the Mountain*, Dutton, 1988 (fiction)

_____ , *The Talking Earth*, HarperCollins, 1983 (fiction)

_____ , *Who Really Killed Cock Robin*, HarperCollins, 1991 (fiction)

Gilbreath, Alice, *The Great Barrier Reef: A Treasure in the Sea*, Dillon, 1986

Goldin, Augusta, *Small Energy Sources: Choices That Work,* Harcourt Brace Jovanovich, 1988

Hadingham, Evan and Janet Hadingham, *Garbage! Where It Comes From, Where It Goes,* Simon and Schuster, 1990

Herberman, Ethan, *The City Kid's Field Guide,* Simon and Schuster, 1989

Hoose, Phillip, *It's Our World, Too! Stories of Young People Who Are Making a Difference,* Little, Brown, 1993

Javna, John, ed., *50 Simple Things Kids Can Do to Save the Earth,* Andrews and McMeel, 1990

Jeffers, Susan, *Brother Eagle, Sister Sky,* Dial, 1991

Jezer, Marty, *Rachel Carson,* Chelsea House, 1988

Johnson, Rebecca L., *The Greenhouse Effect: Life on a Warmer Planet,* Lerner, 1990

Kronenwetter, Michael, *Managing Toxic Wastes,* Messner, 1989

Landau, Elaine, *Tropical Rain Forests Around the World,* Franklin Watts, 1990

Leinwand, Gerald, *The Environment,* Facts on File, 1990

Lewis, Barbara, *A Kid's Guide to Social Action: How to Solve the Social Problems You Choose—And Turn Creative Thinking into Positive Action,* Free Spirit, 1991

McLaughlin, Molly, *Earthworms, Dirt and Rotten Leaves: An Exploration in Ecology,* Macmillan, 1986

Middleton, Nick, *Atlas of Environmental Issues,* Facts on File, 1993

Miller, Christina G. and Louise A. Berry, *Acid Rain: A Sourcebook for Young People,* Messner, 1986

_____ , *Coastal Rescue: Preserving Our Seashores,* Macmillan, 1989

Newton, David E., *Taking a Stand Against Environmental Pollution,* Franklin Watts, 1990

Norsgaard, E. Jaediker, *Nature's Great Balancing Act: In Our Own Back Yard,* Dutton, 1990

O'Connor, Karen, *Garbage*, Lucent, 1989

Parker, Steve, *Pond and River*, Knopf, 1988

_____ , *Seashore*, Knopf, 1989

Pollack, Steve, *Atlas of Endangered Animals*, Facts on File, 1993

_____ , *Atlas of Endangered Places*, Facts on File, 1993

Pringle, Laurence, *Living Treasure: Saving Earth's Threatened Biodiversity*, Morrow, 1991

_____ , *Nuclear Energy: Troubled Past, Uncertain Future*, Macmillan, 1989

_____ , *Restoring Our Earth*, Enslow, 1987

Robinson, David F., ed., *Living on the Earth*, National Geographic, 1988

Schwartz, Linda, *Earth Book for Kids: Activities to Help Heal the Environment*, Learning Works, 1990

Shaffer, Carolyn and Erica Fielder, *City Safaris: A Sierra Club Explorer's Guide to Urban Adventures for Grownups and Kids*, Sierra Club, 1987

Sharpe, Susan, *Trouble at Marsh Harbor*, Puffin Books, 1990 (fiction)

Stone, Lynn M., *Wetlands*, Rourke, 1989

Tesar, Jenny E., *Global Warming*, Facts on File, 1991

BOOKS FOR ADULTS

Carson, Rachel, *The Sea Around Us*, New American Library, 1954

_____ , *The Sense of Wonder*, Harper, 1987

_____ , *Silent Spring*, Houghton Mifflin, 1962

Ehrlich, Paul R. and Anne H. Ehrlich, *Healing the Planet: Strategies for Resolving the Environmental Crisis*, Addison-Wesley, 1991

Fossey, Diane, *Gorillas in the Mist,* Houghton Mifflin, 1988

Gore, Albert, Jr., *Earth in the Balance,* Houghton Mifflin, 1992

Lippson, Alice Jane and Robert L. Lippson, *Life in the Chesapeake Bay,* Johns Hopkins University Press, 1984

MacEachern, Diane, *Save Our Planet: 750 Everyday Ways You Can Help Clean Up the Earth,* Dell, 1990

McPhee, John, *Encounters with the Archdruid,* Farrar, Straus and Giroux, 1971

Mowat, Farley, *Never Cry Wolf,* Bantam, 1979

_____ , *A Whale for the Killing,* Bantam, 1981

Myers, Norman, ed., *Gaia: An Atlas of Planet Management,* Anchor/Doubleday, 1984

Rathje, William and Cullen Murphy, *Rubbish! The Archaeology of Garbage,* HarperCollins, 1992

Schumacher, E. F., *Small Is Beautiful: Economics As If People Mattered,* Harper, 1973

Sinclair, Patti K., *E for Environment: An Annotated Bibliography of Children's Books with Environmental Themes,* Bowker, 1992

Storer, John H., *The Web of Life,* New American Library, 1953

Thoreau, Henry David, *Walden; or, Life in the Woods,* Anchor/Doubleday, 1973

Warner, William, *Beautiful Swimmers,* Little, 1976

Wilson, Edward O., *The Diversity of Life,* Harvard University Press, 1992

World Resources Institute, *The Information Please Environmental Almanac,* Houghton Mifflin

INDEX

223